FUCK

By the same author

Graphic Novels
The Waste Land
Tristram Shandy

Fiction
Snatches

Non-Fiction
Stuff
The Dog Allusion

FUCK
The Human Odyssey

Martin Rowson

JONATHAN CAPE
LONDON

Published by Jonathan Cape 2008

2 4 6 8 10 9 7 5 3 1

First published in Great Britain in 2008 by
Jonathan Cape
Random House, 20 Vauxhall Bridge Road,
London SW1V 2SA

The Random House Group Limited Reg. No. 954009

A CIP catalogue record for this book is available from the British Library

ISBN 9780224084413

The Random House Group Limited makes every effort to ensure that the papers used in its books
are made from trees that have been legally sourced from well-managed and credibly certified forests.
Our paper procurement policy can be found at: www.randomhouse.co.uk/paper.htm

Colour reproduction by XY Digital Ltd, London, Great Britain
Printed and bound in China by C&C Offset Printing Co., Ltd

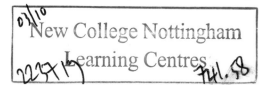

As ever, for Anna, Fred and Rose

The Big Bang

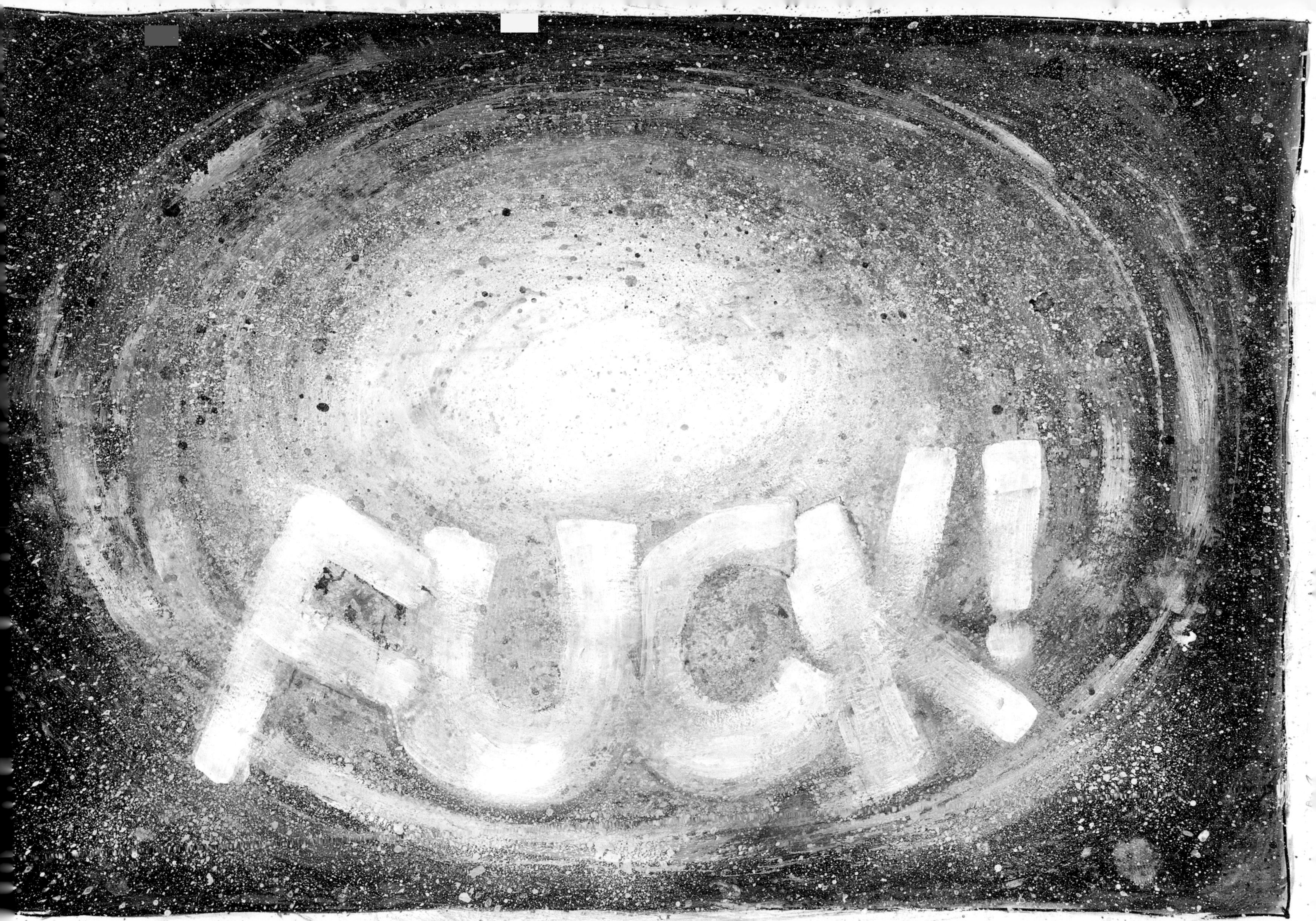
FUCK!

The Formation of the Solar System

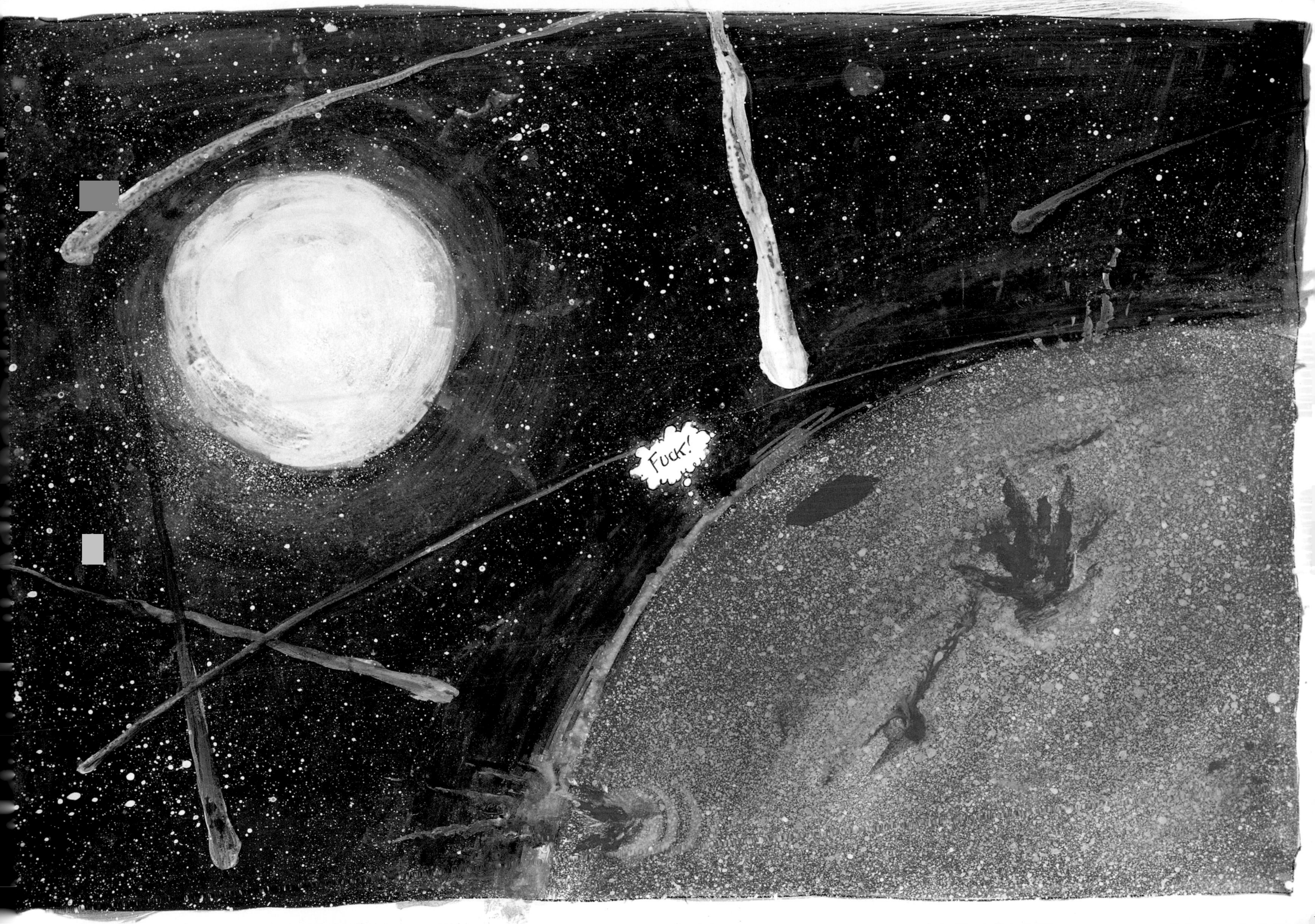
FUCK!

The Birth of Life

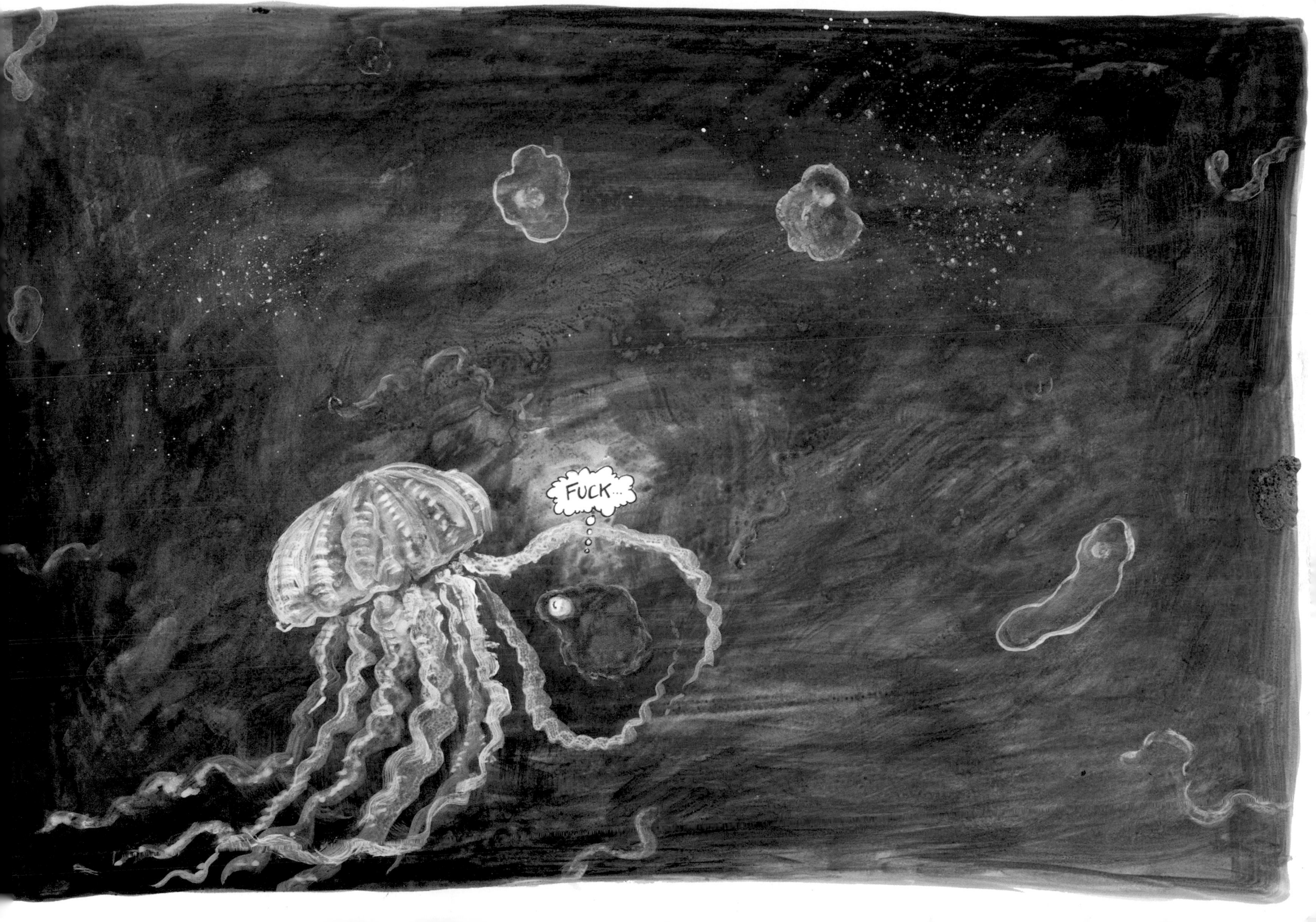
FUCK...

The Conquest of the Land

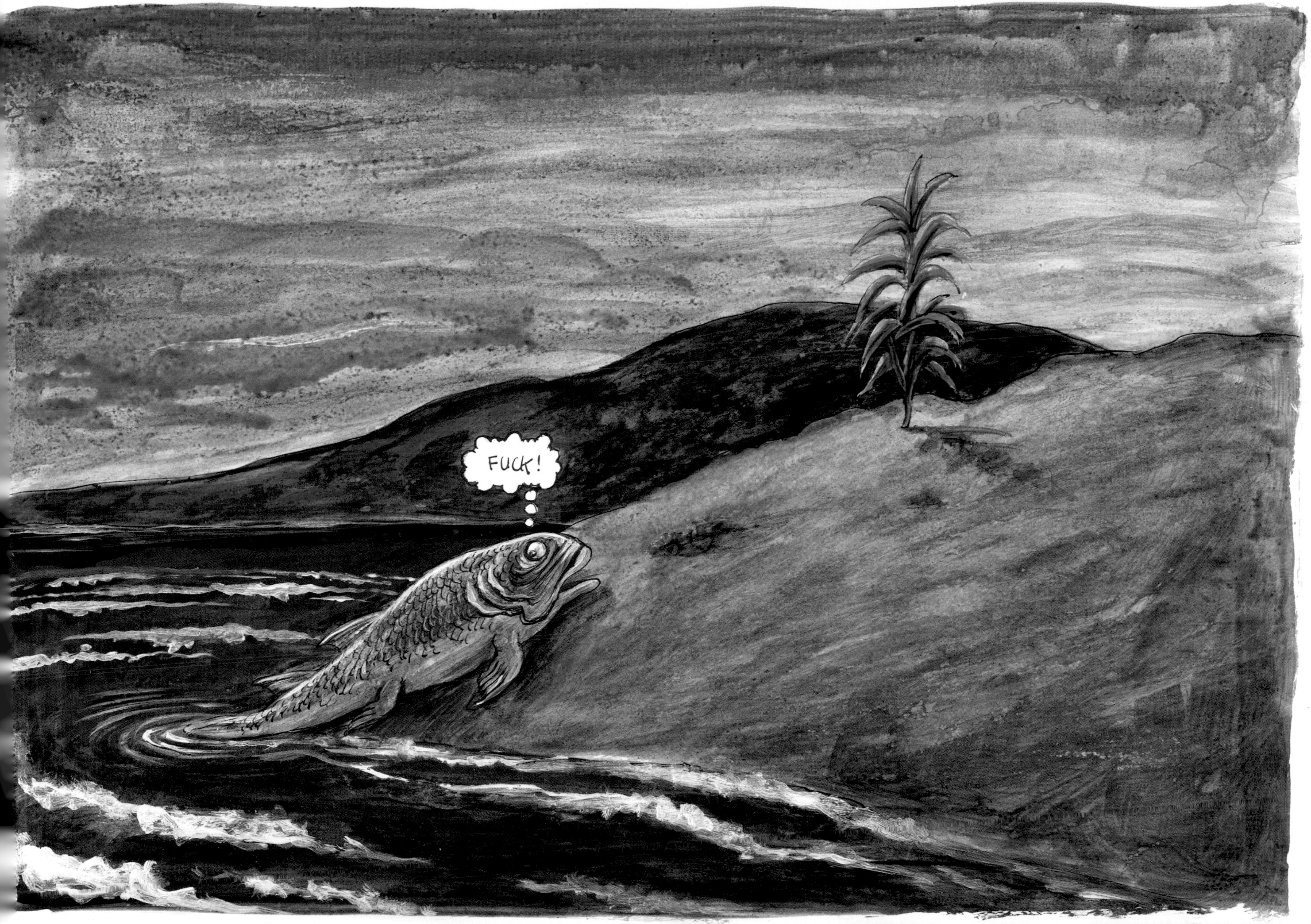
FUCK!

Dinosaurs Rule the Earth

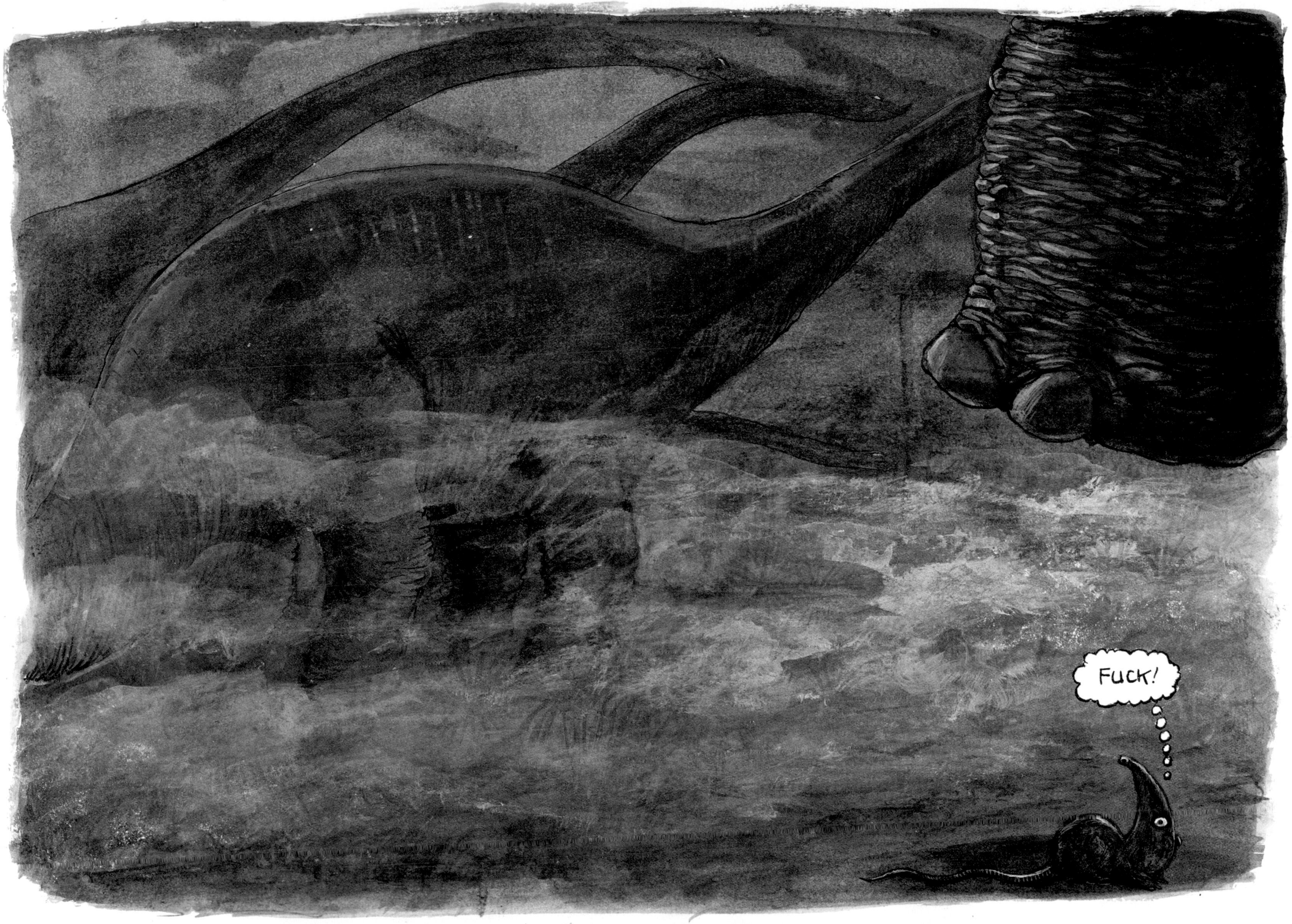
FUCK!

The Extinction of the Dinosaurs

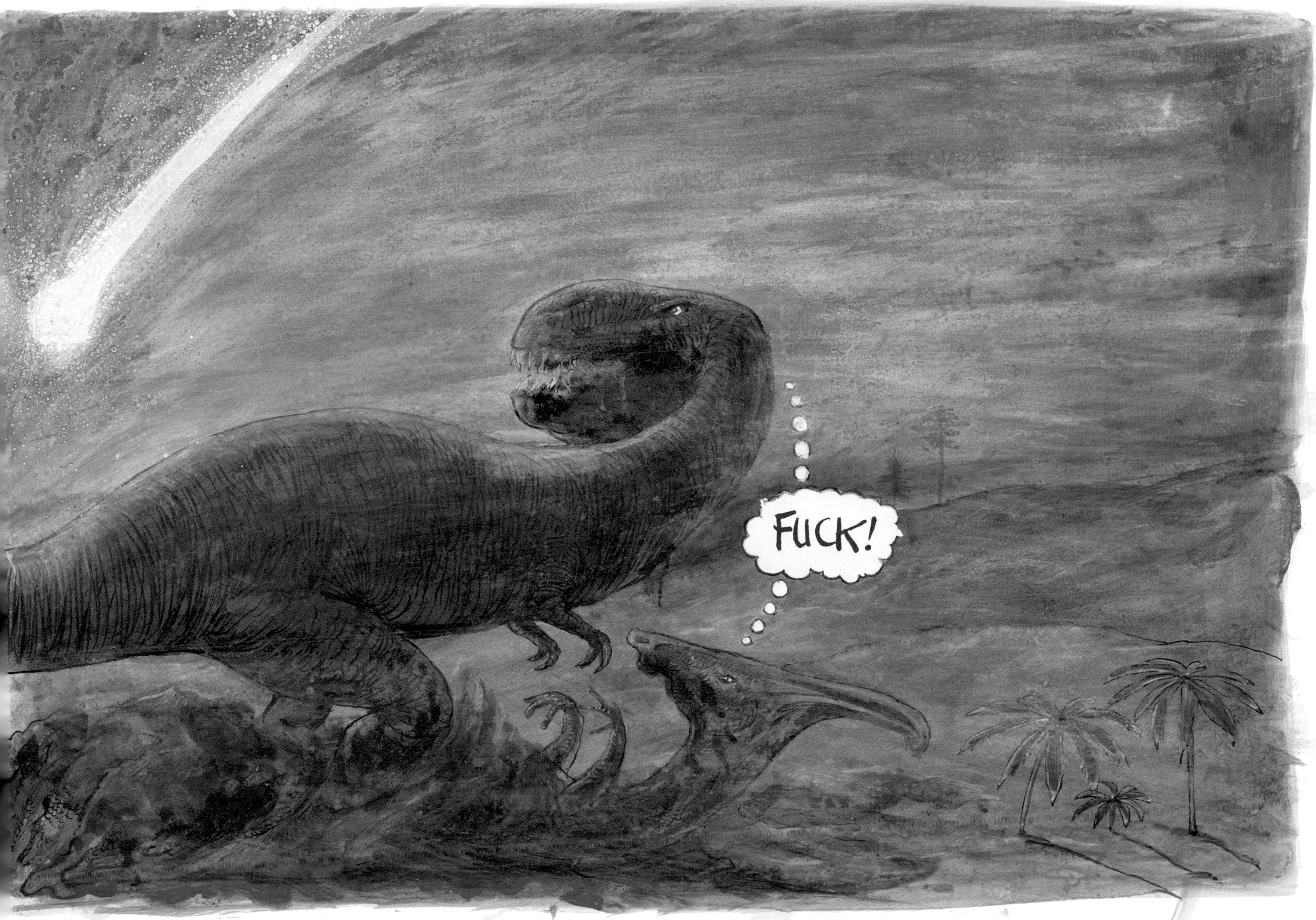
FUCK!

The Miracle of Bipedalism

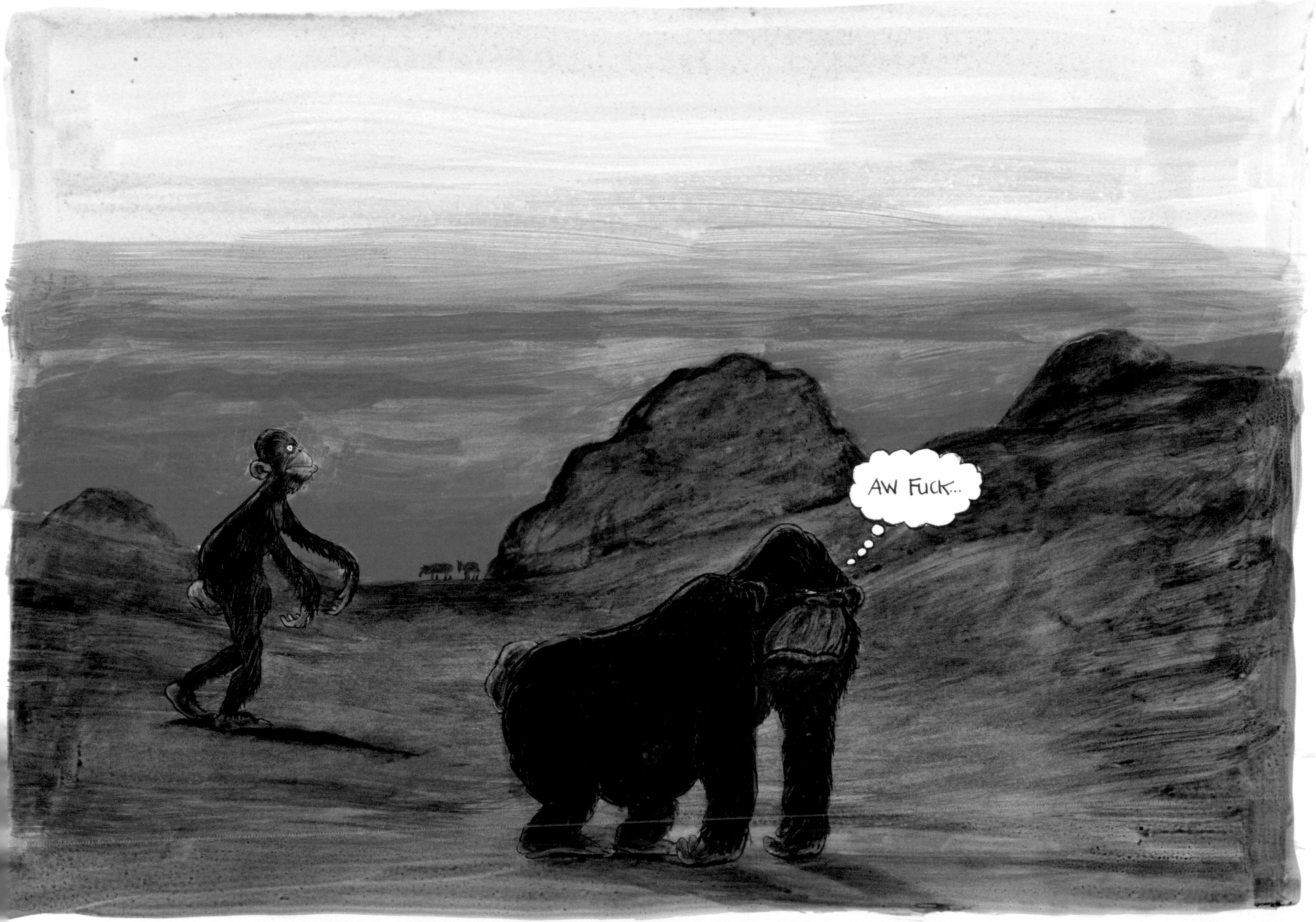
AW FUCK...

The Acquisition of Tools

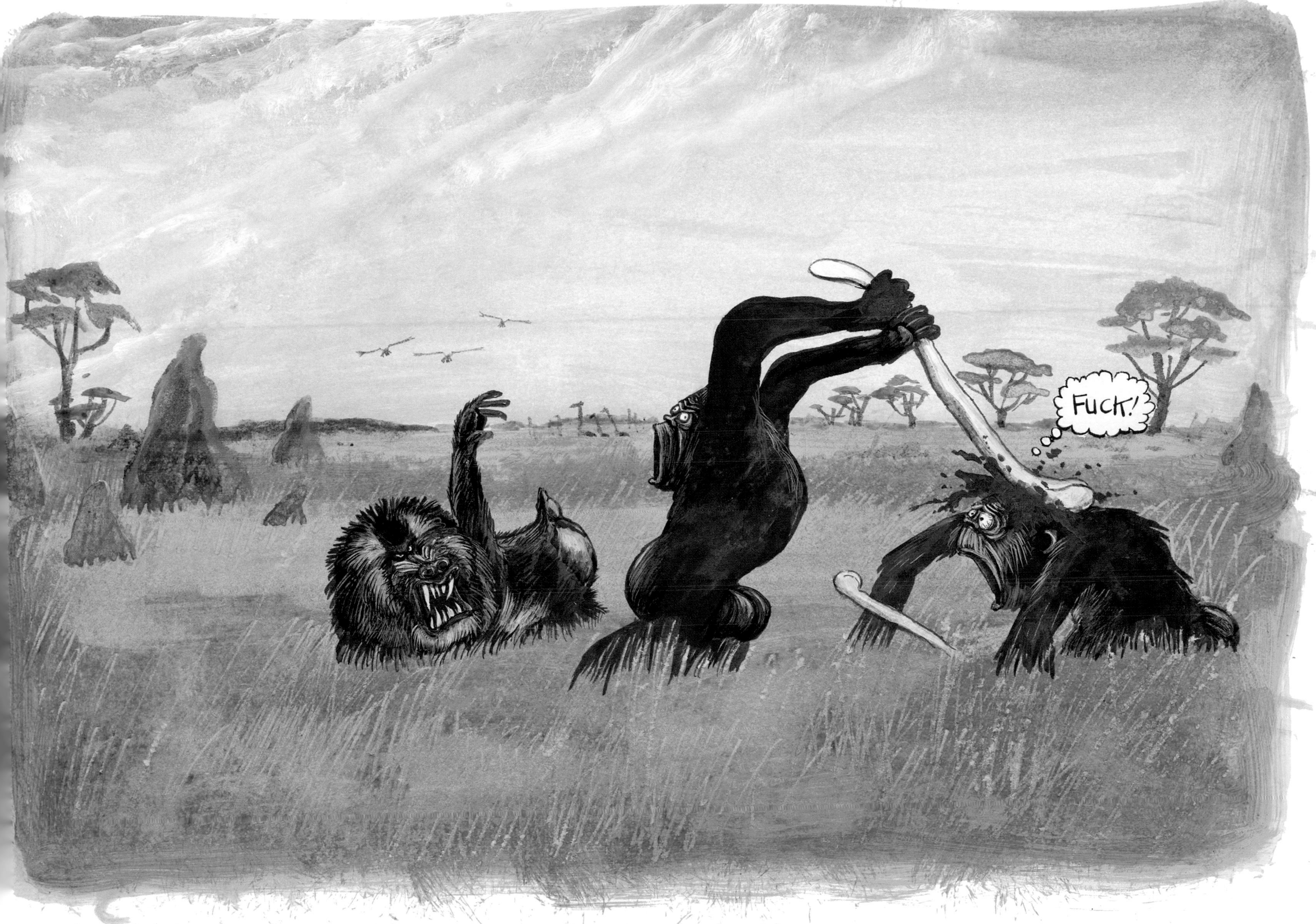
FUCK!

The Birth of Language

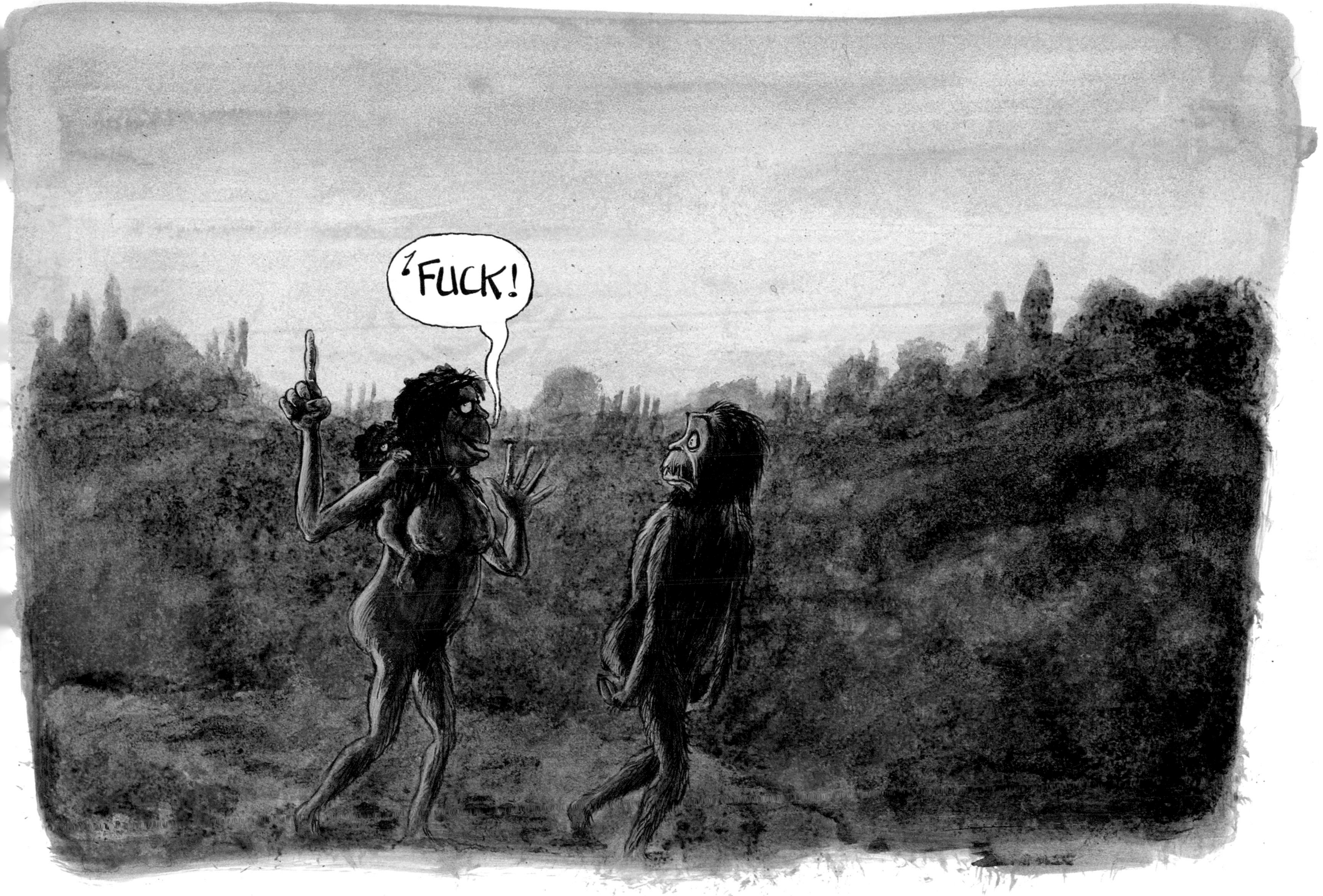
'FUCK!

The Neanderthals Die Out

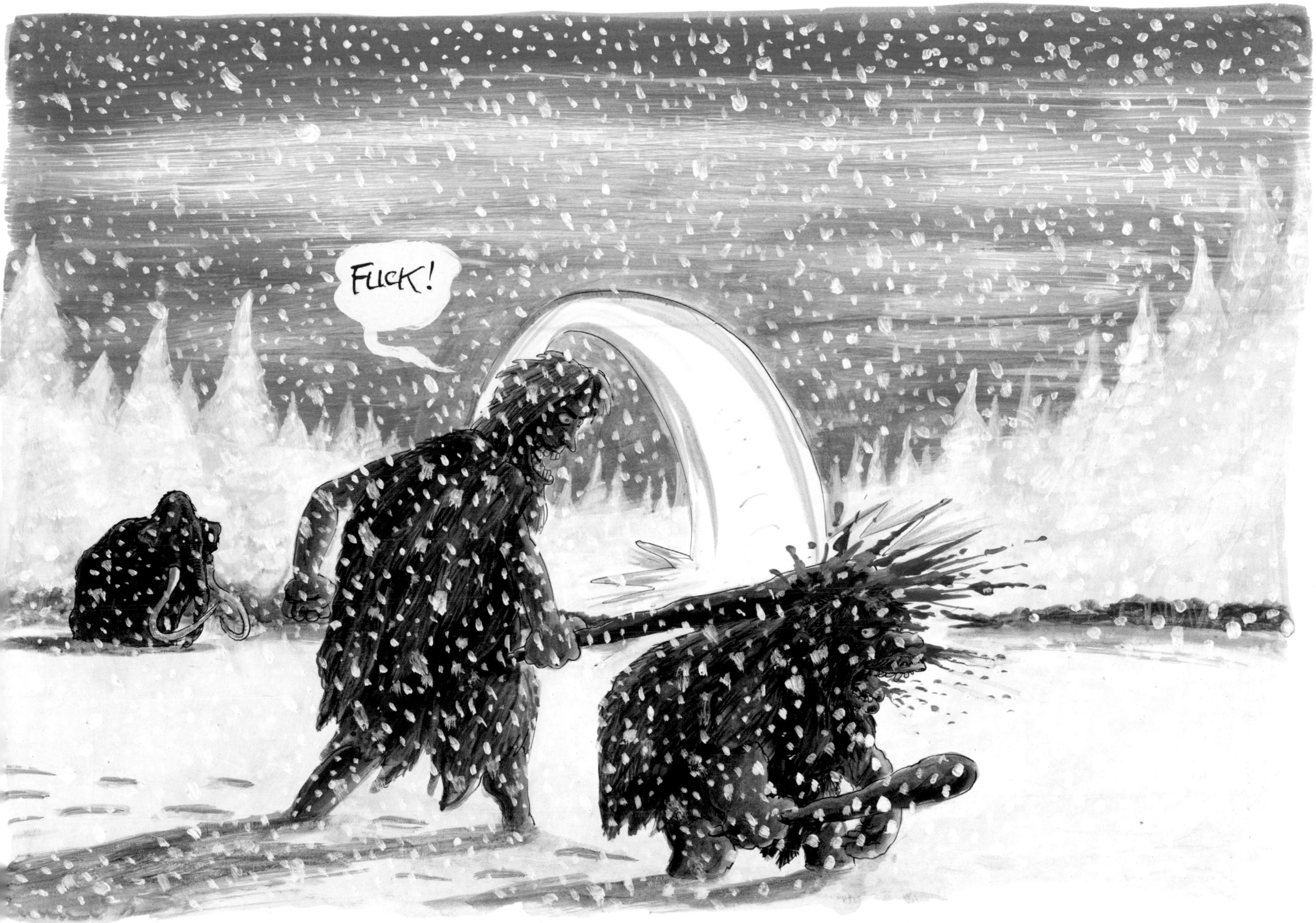
FUCK!

The Invention of the Wheel

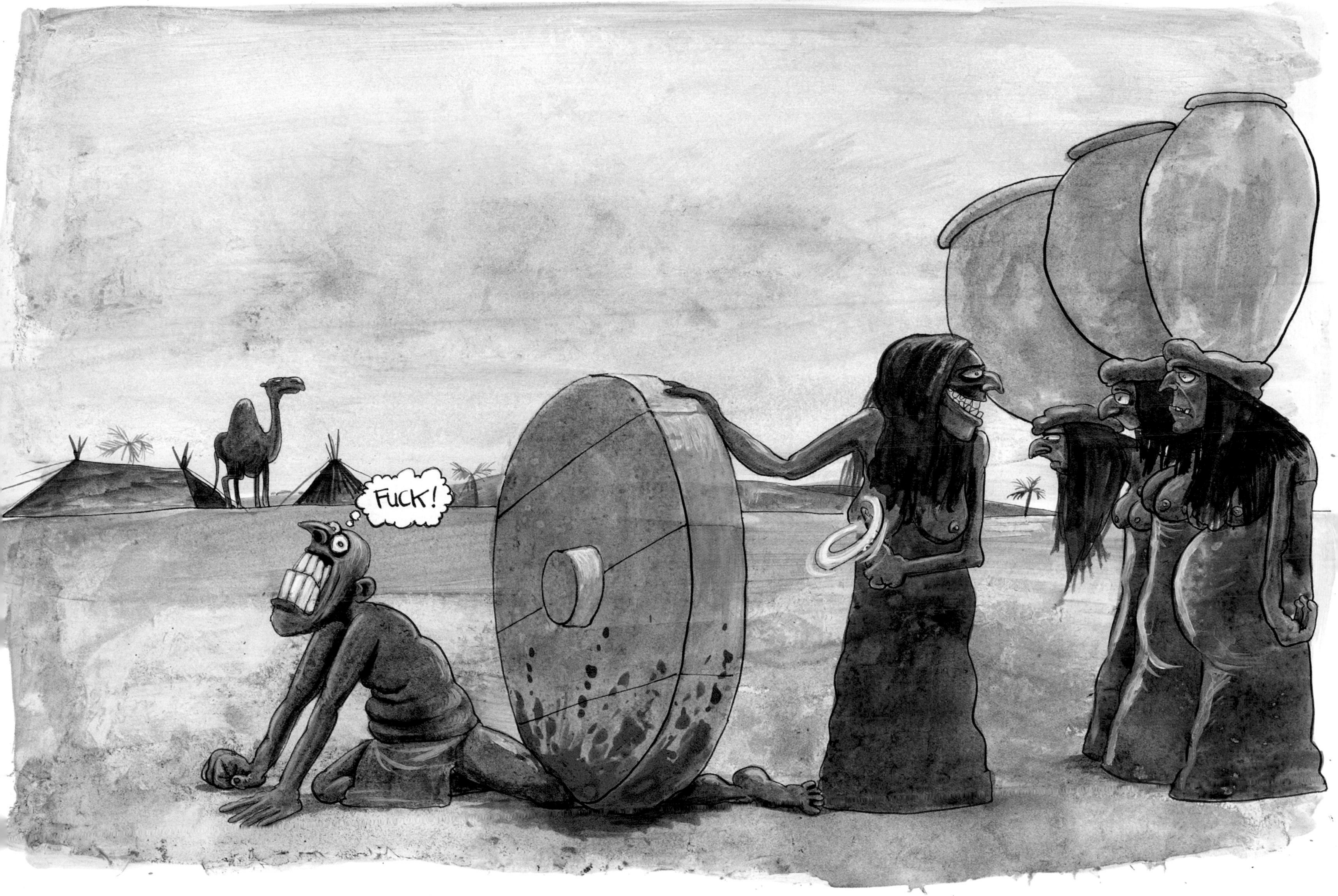
FUCK!

Agriculture

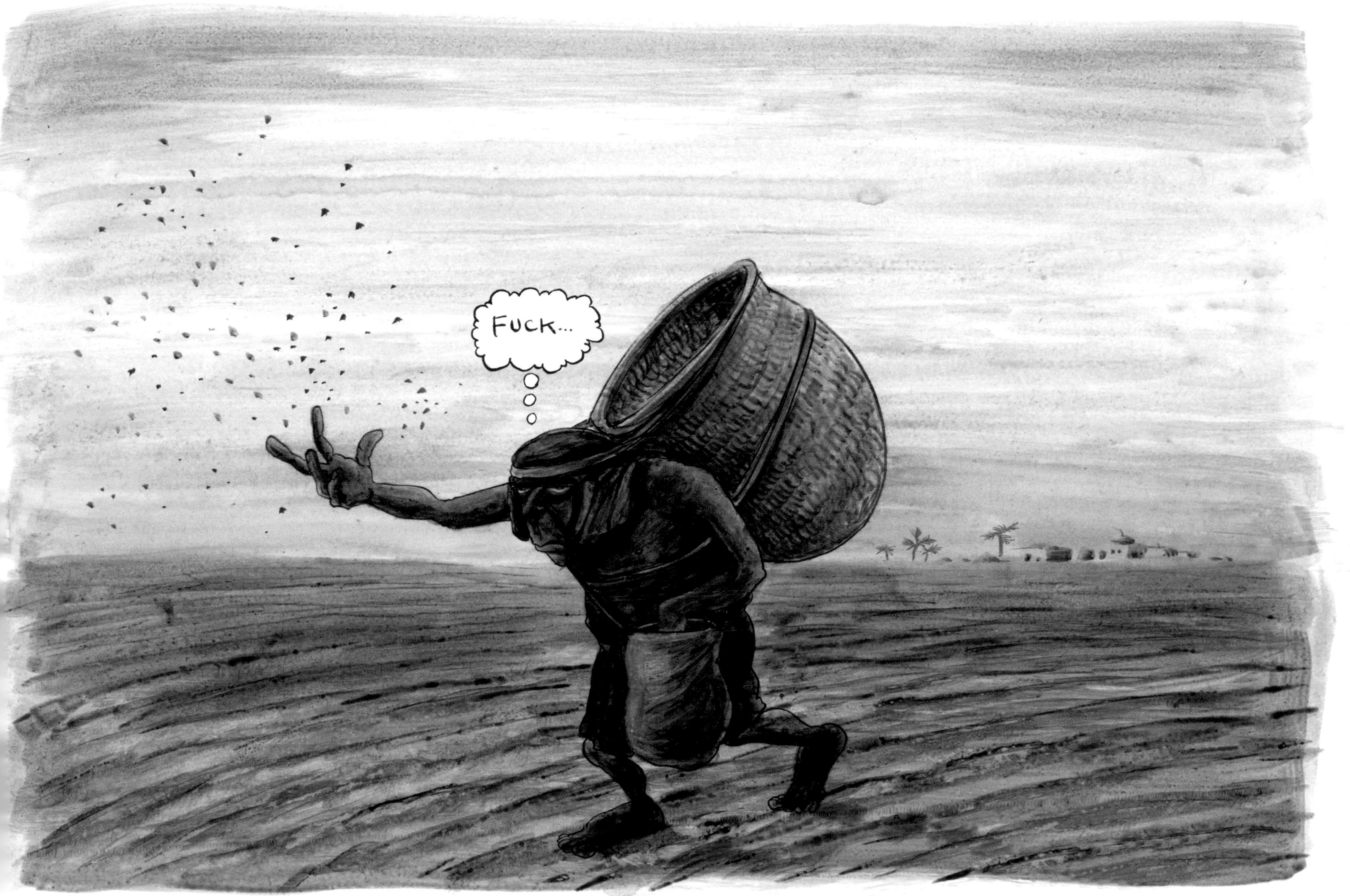
FUCK...

The Development of Writing

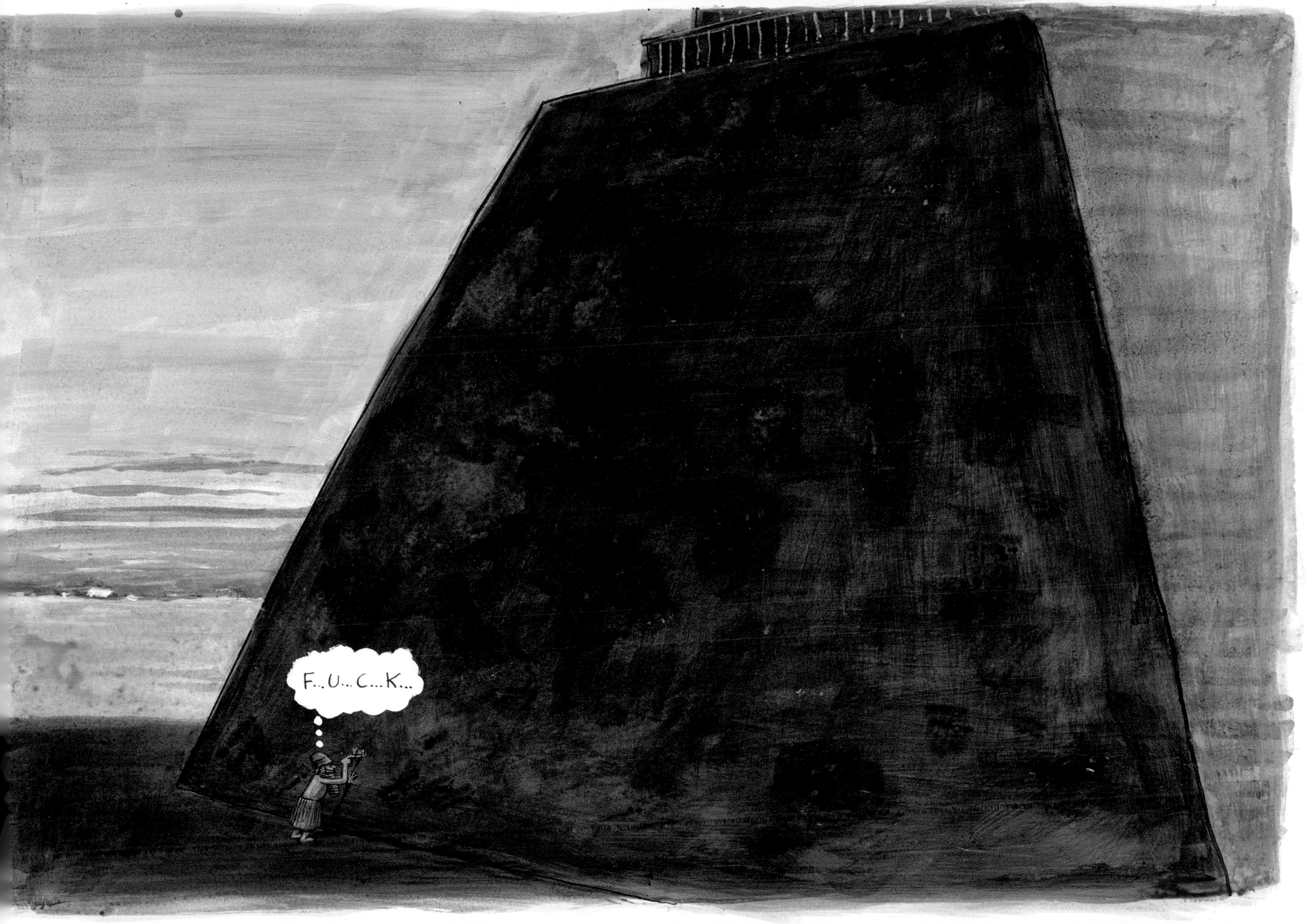
F...U...C...K...

The Siege of Troy

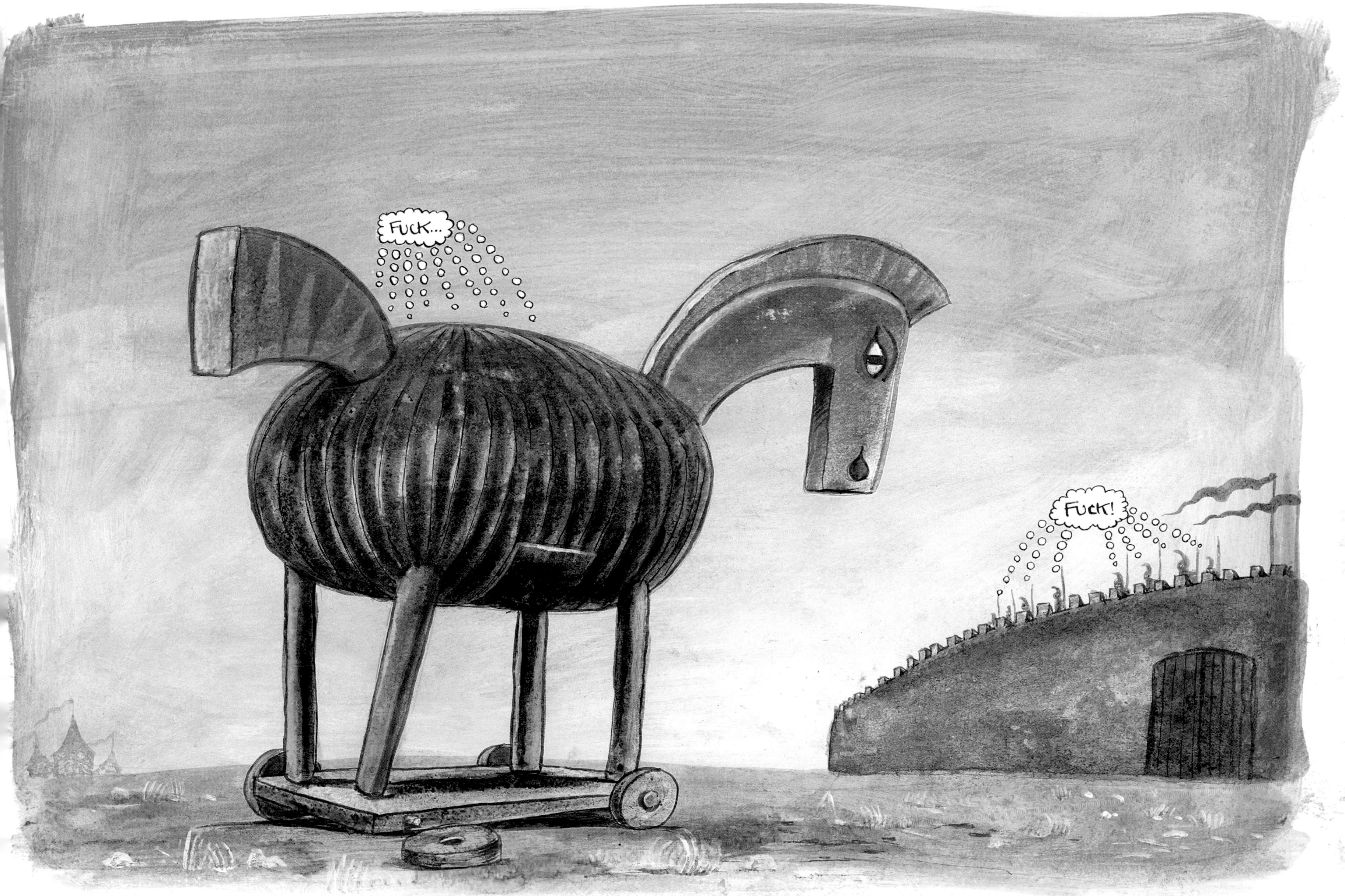
FUCK...
FUCK!

The Ten Commandments

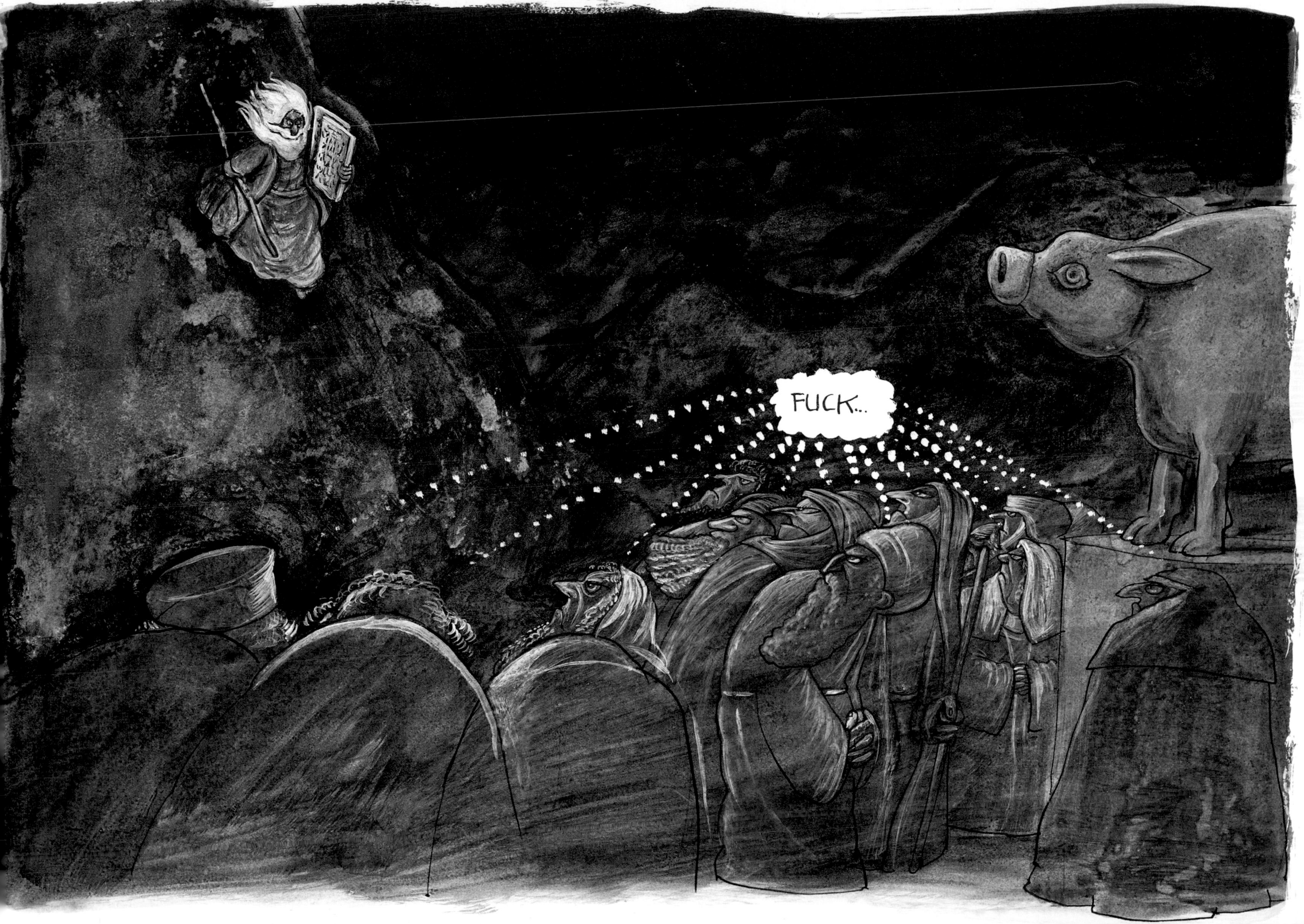
FUCK...

Athenian Philosophy

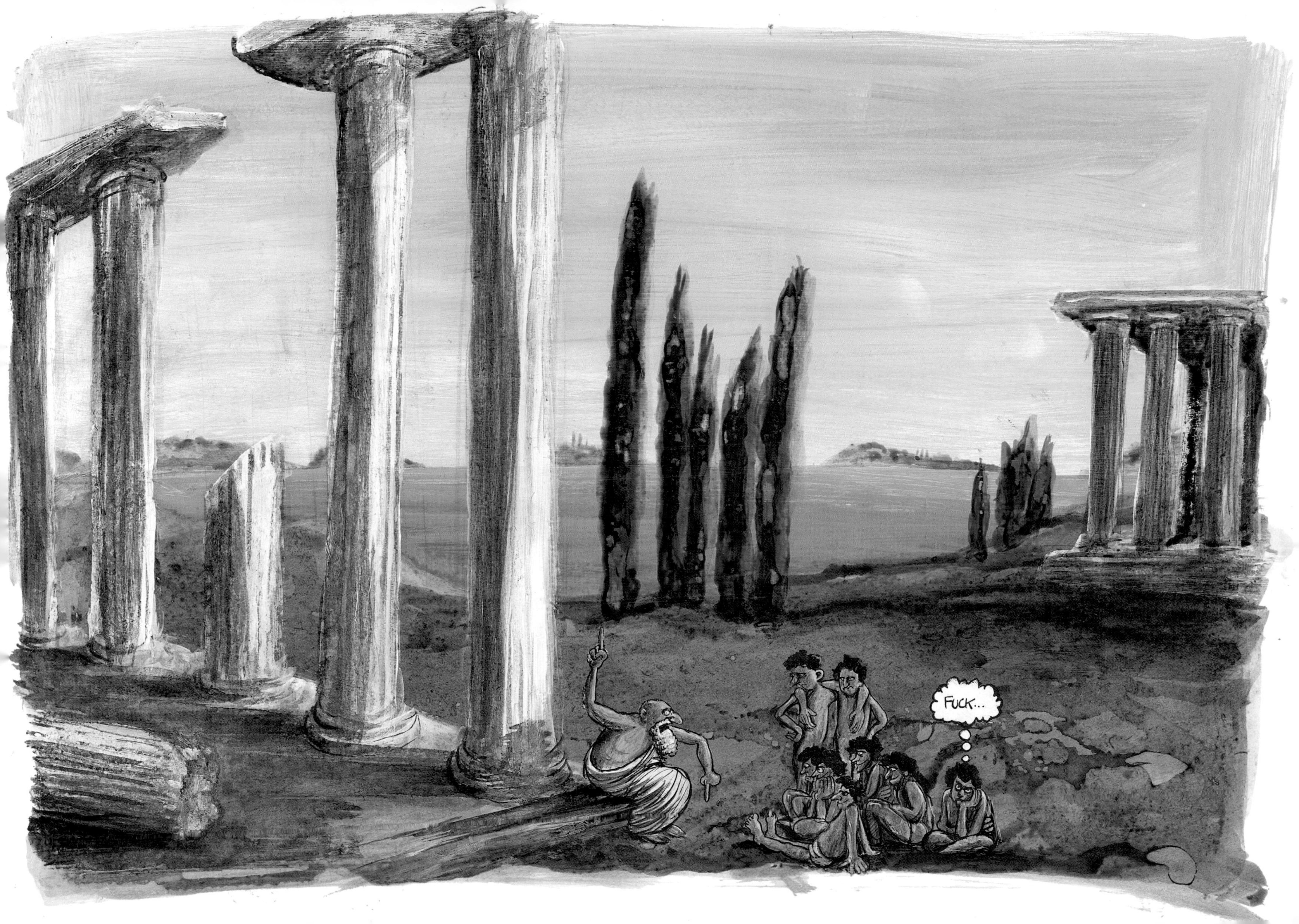
FUCK...

The Birth of the Drama

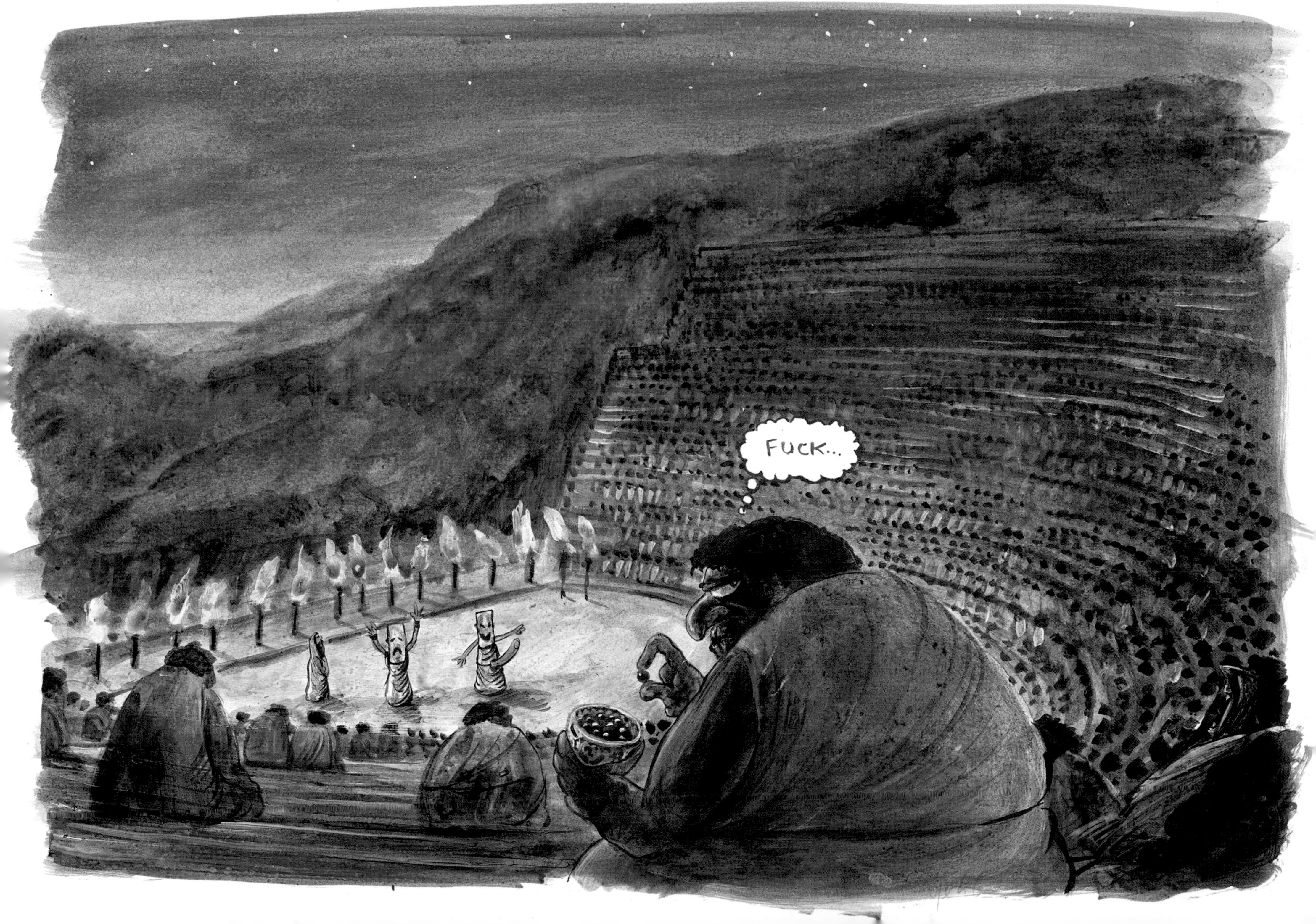
FUCK...

Archimedes

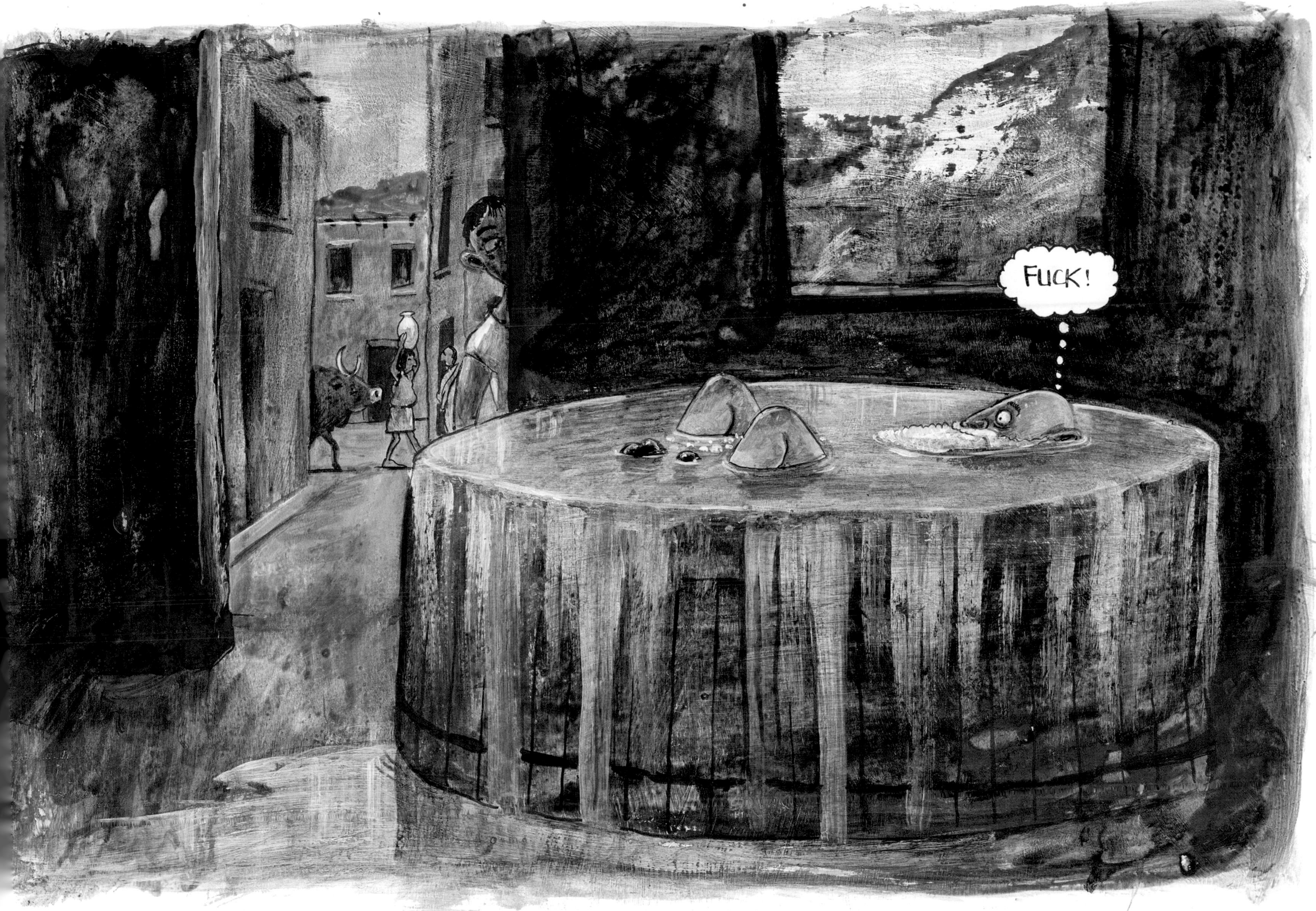
FUCK!

The Adoration of the Magi

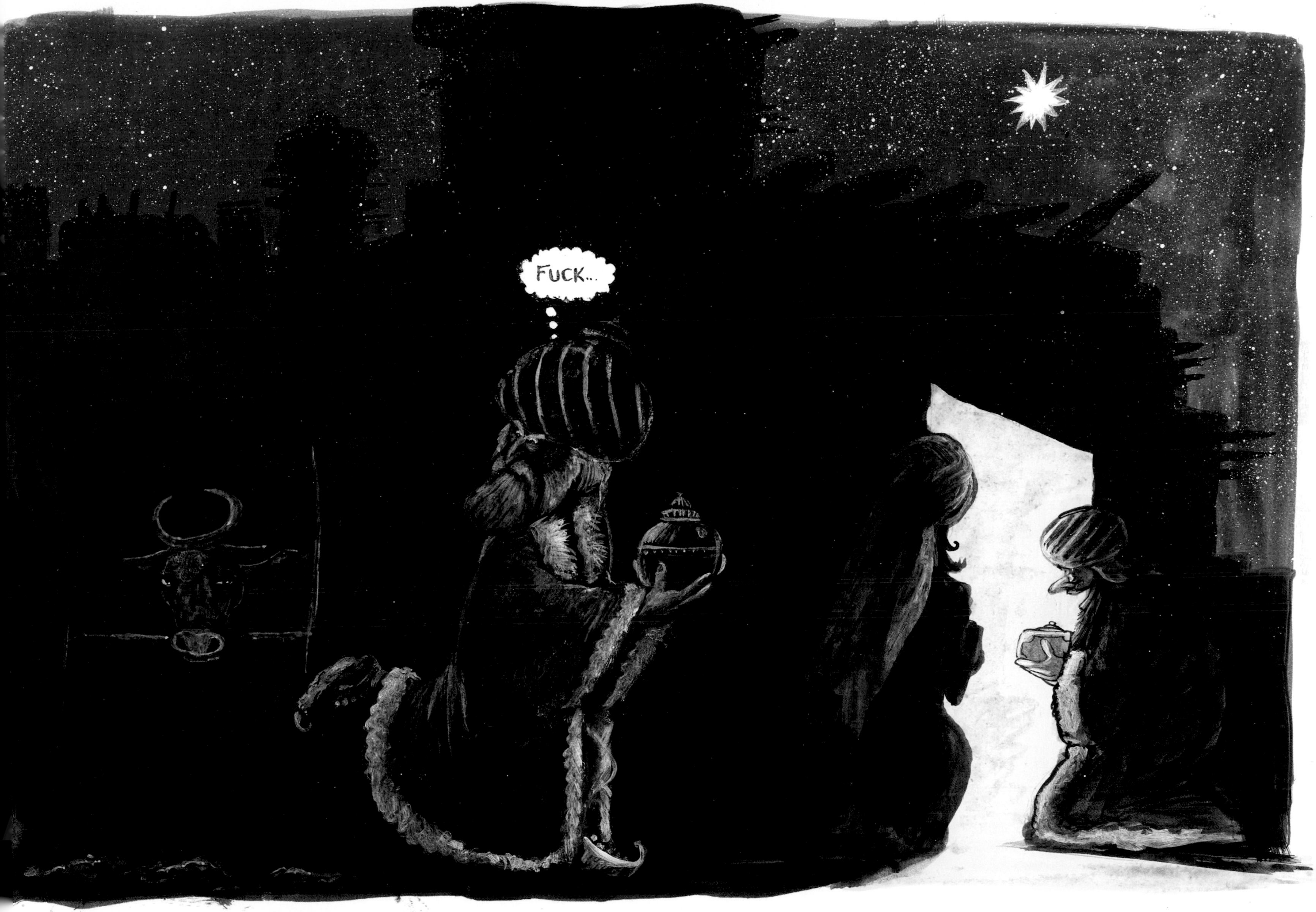
FUCK...

The Passion of our Lord

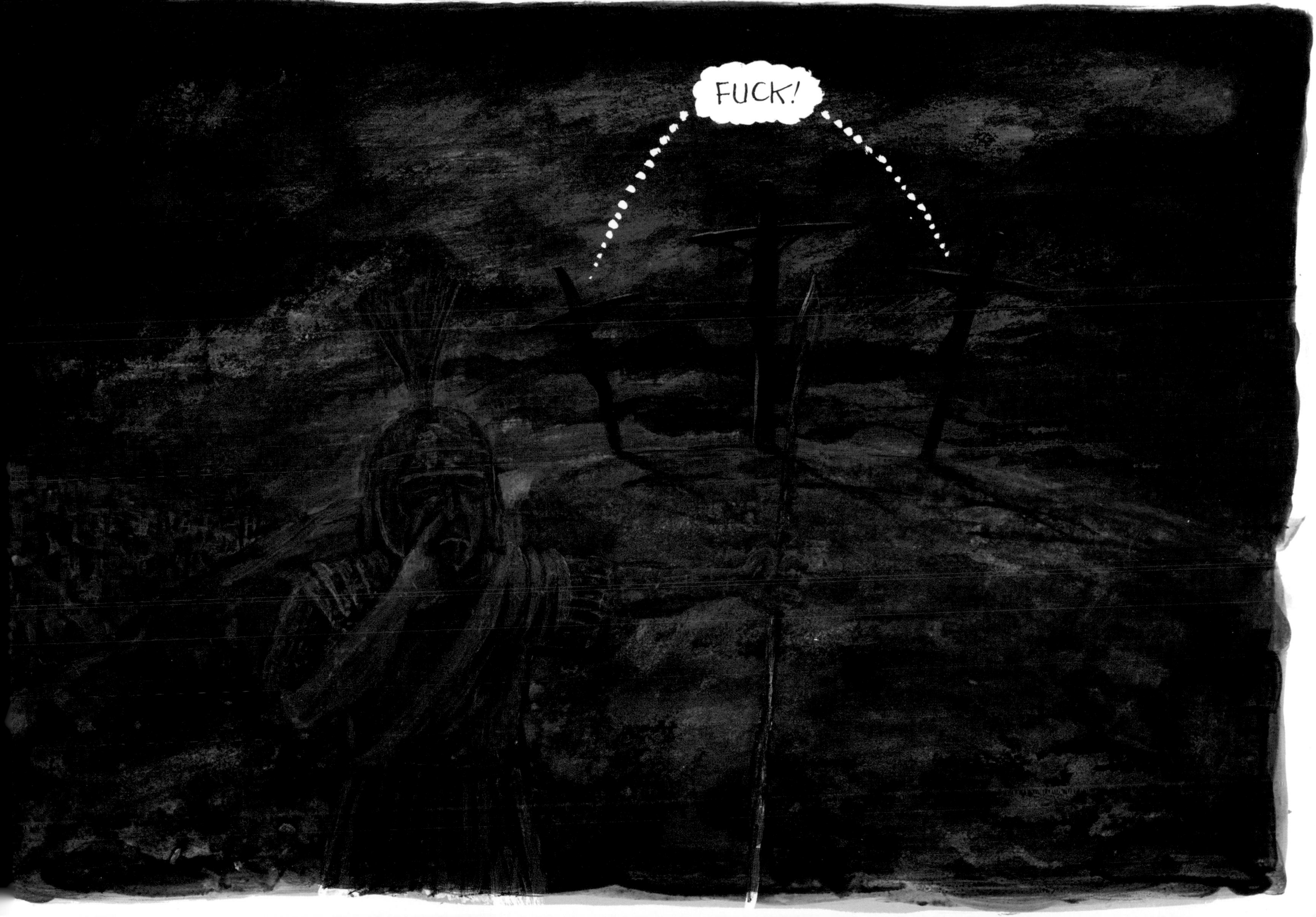
FUCK!

The Decline and Fall of the Roman Empire

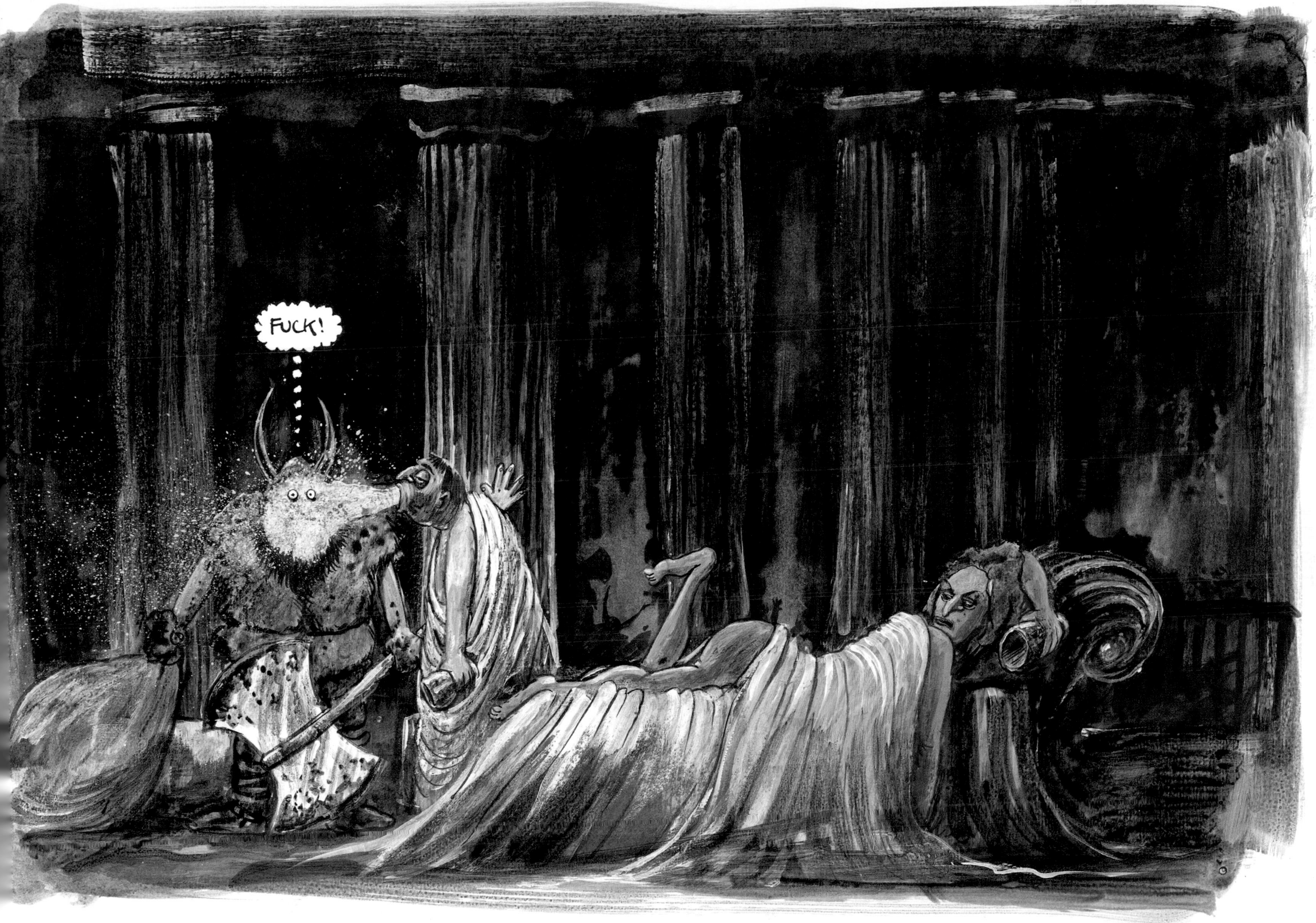
FUCK!

Monasticism Keeps Learning Alive through the Dark Ages

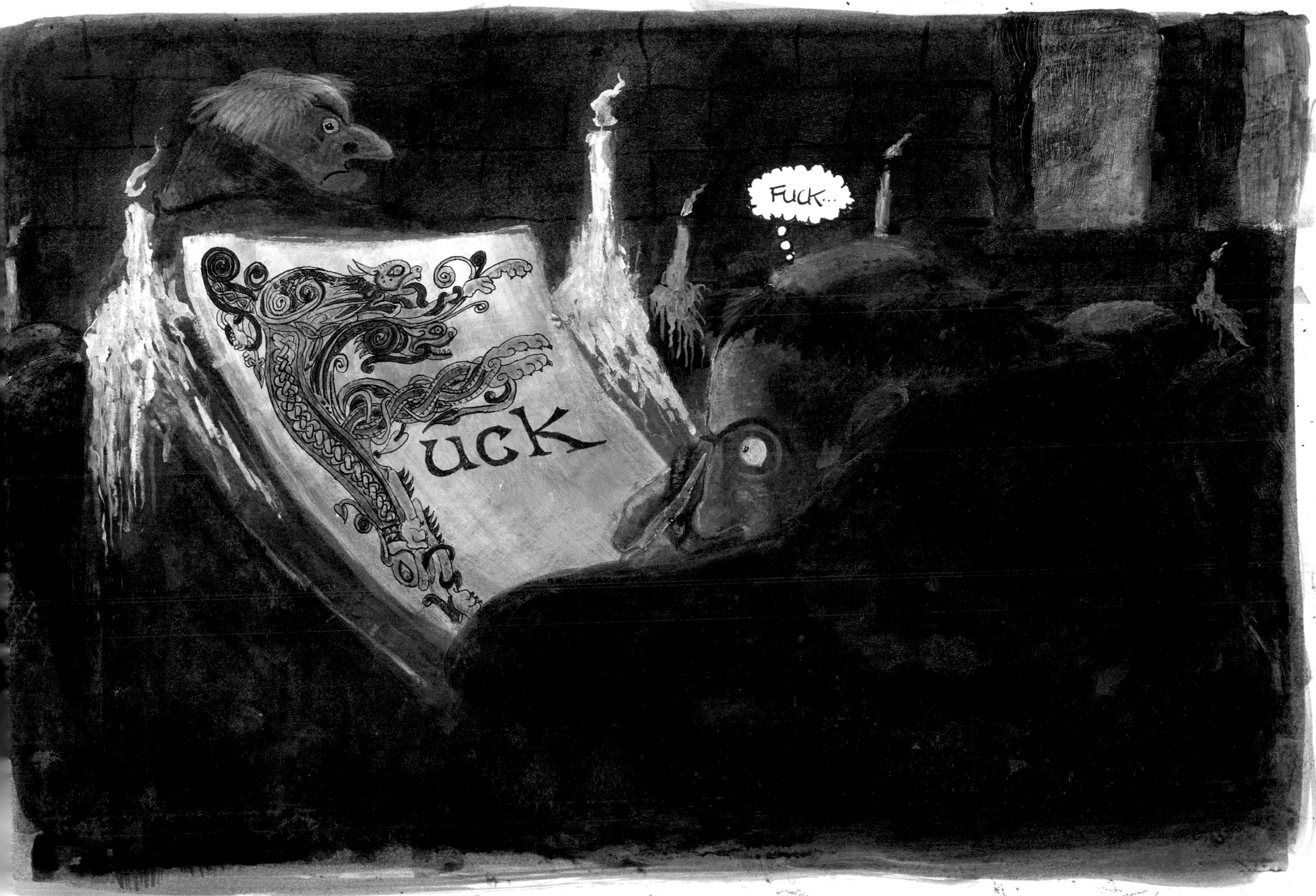
FUCK...
UCK

The Vikings

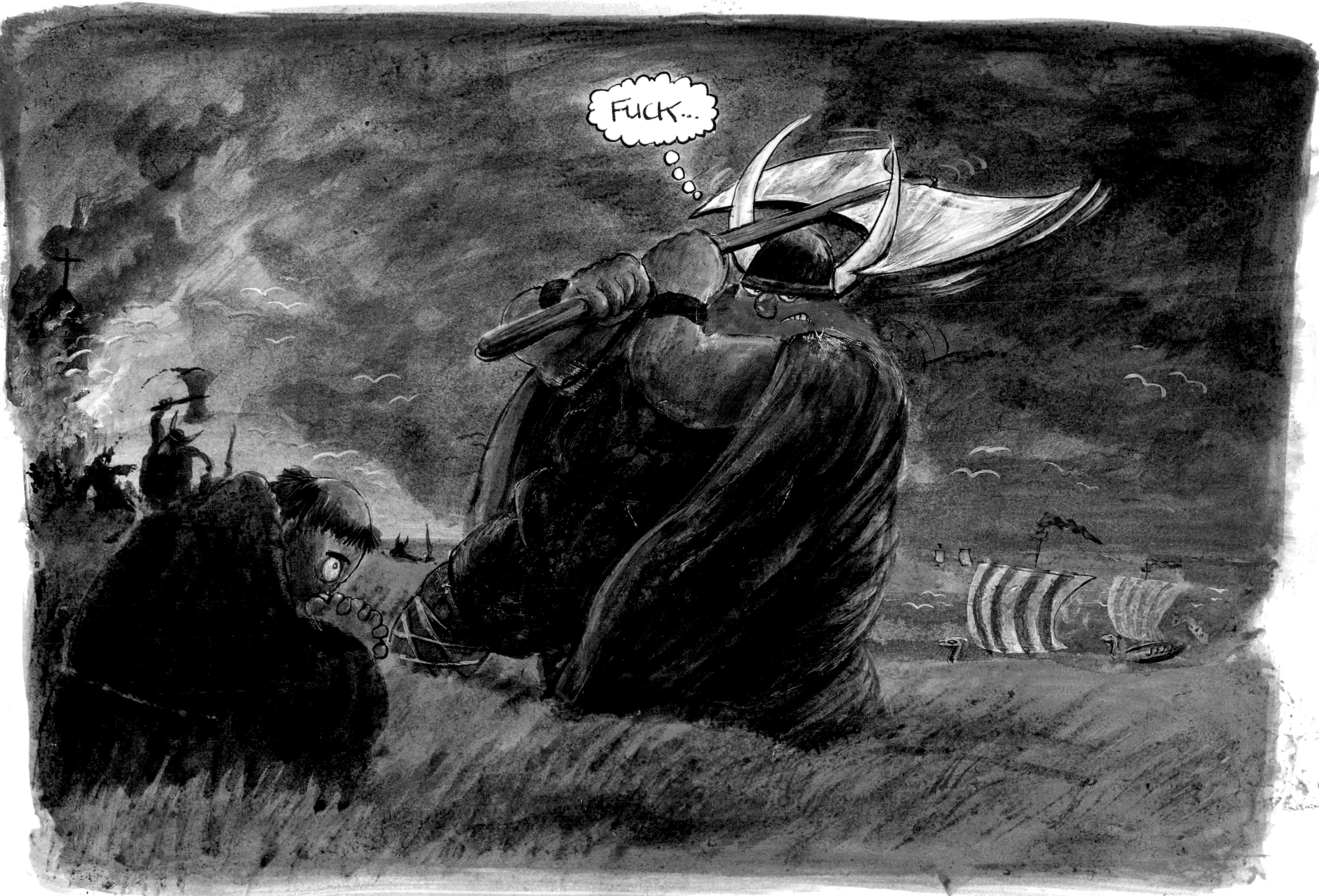
FUCK...

The Age of Chivalry

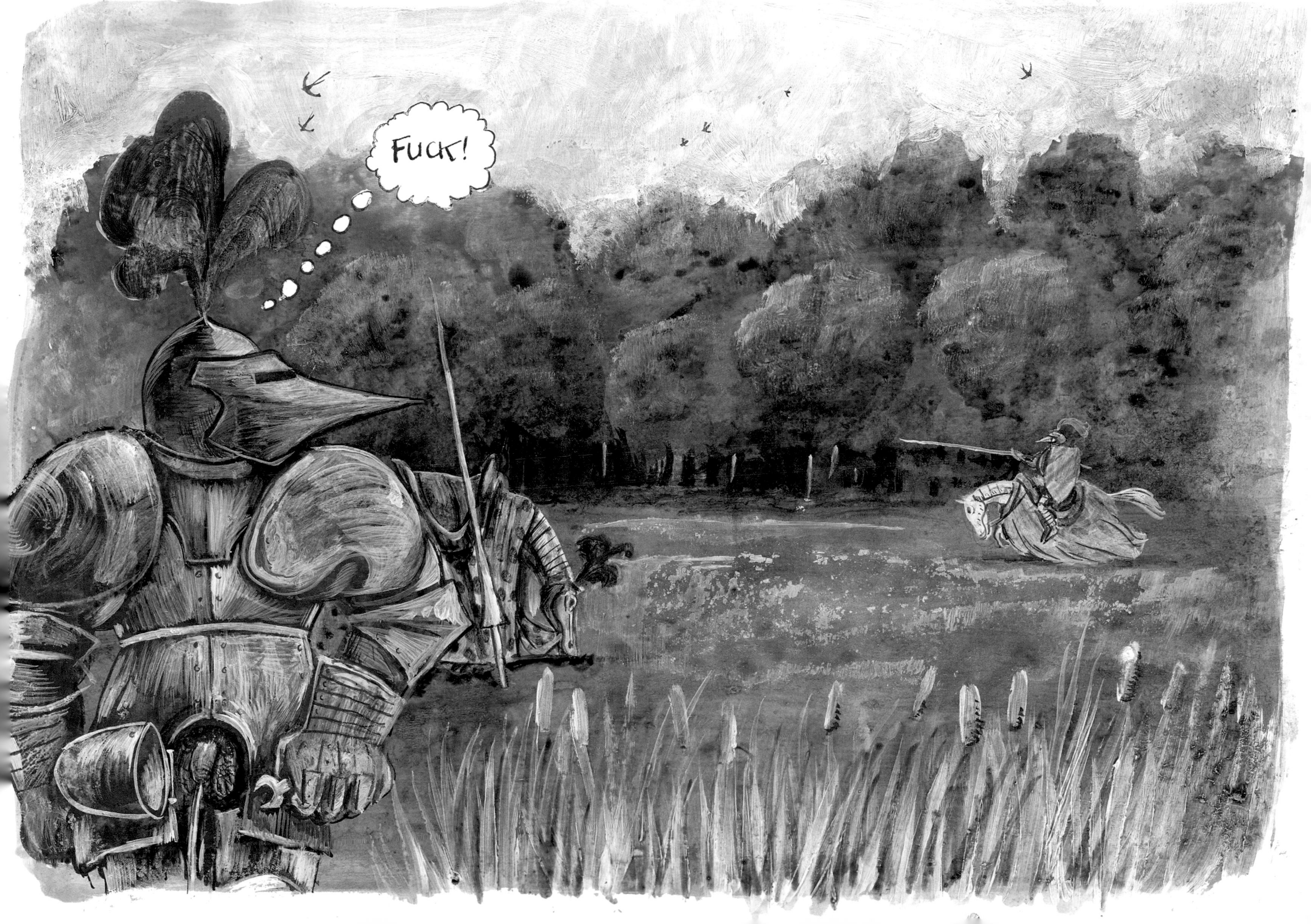
FUCK!

The Black Death

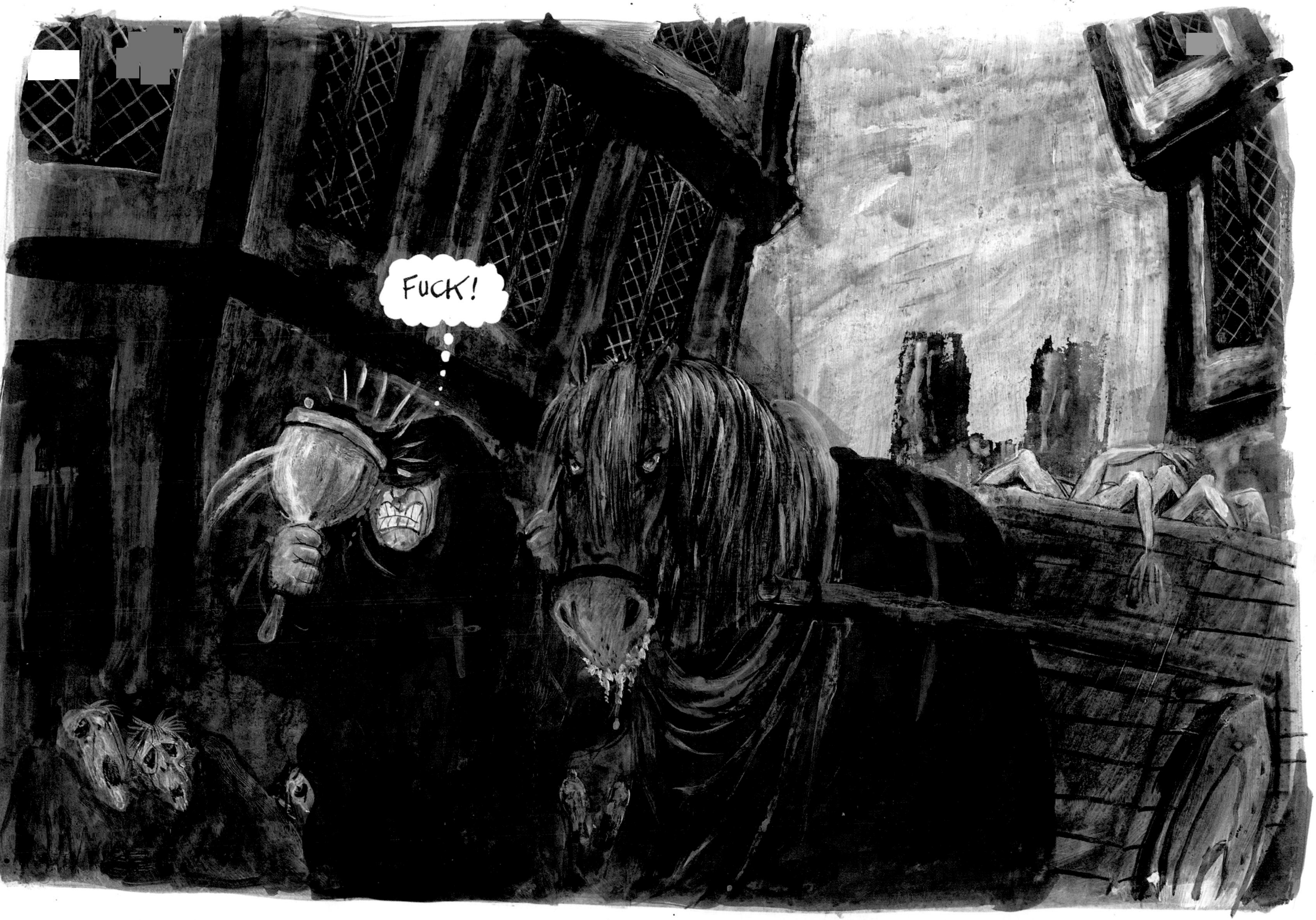
FUCK!

Chaucer's Canterbury Pilgrims

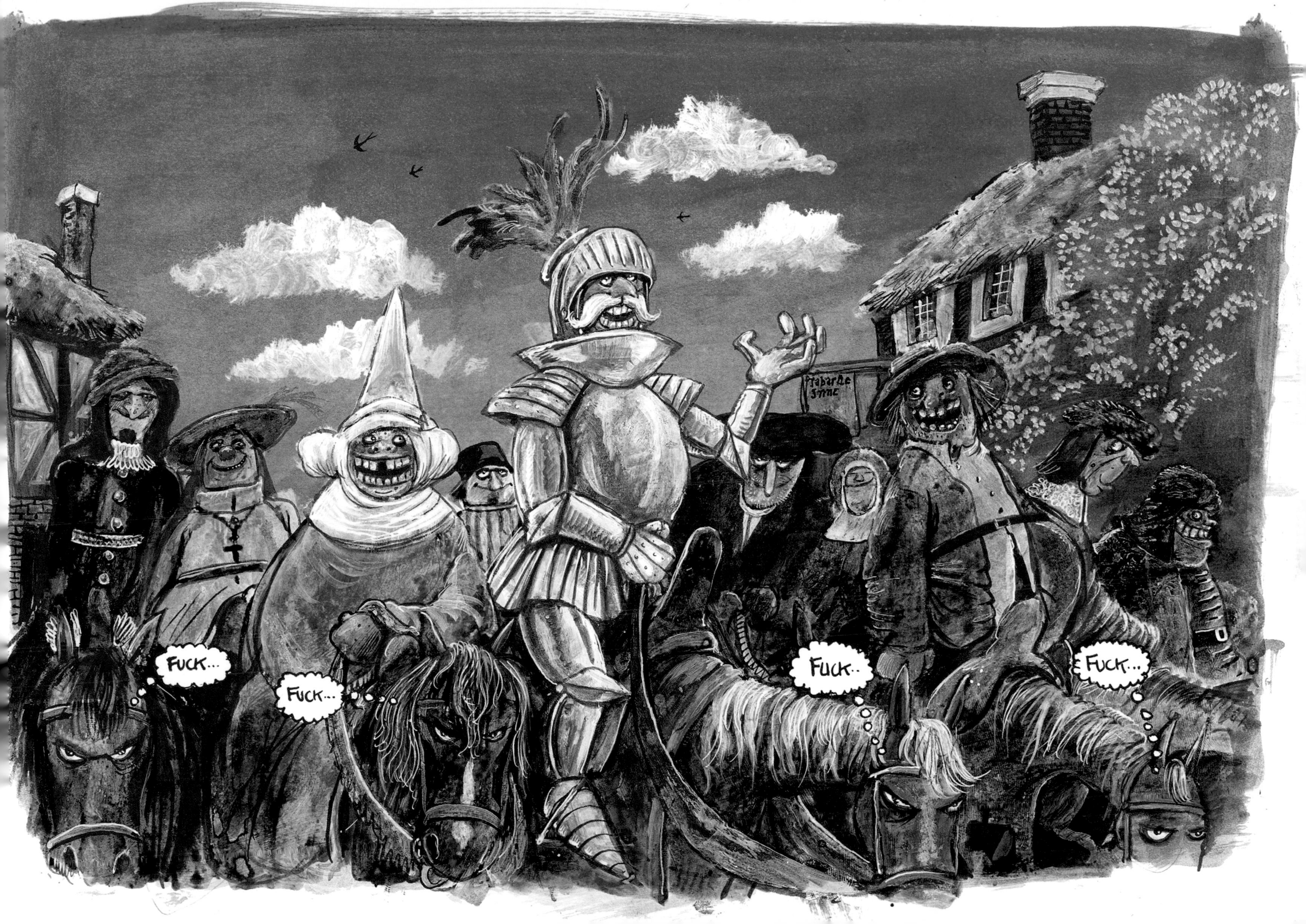

Tabarde
Inne
FUCK...
FUCK...
FUCK..
FUCK...

The Invention of Printing

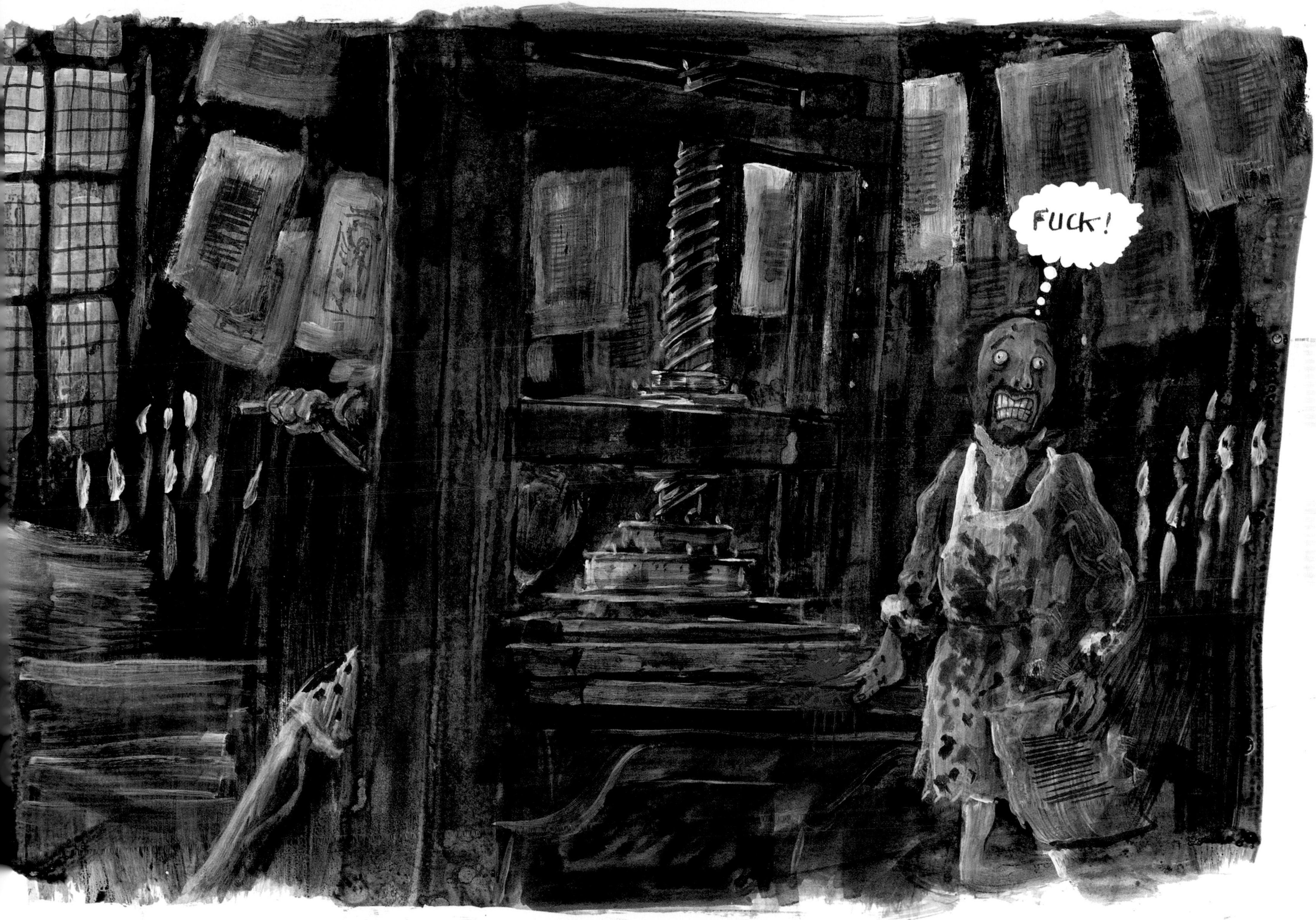
FUCK!

The Discovery of the New World

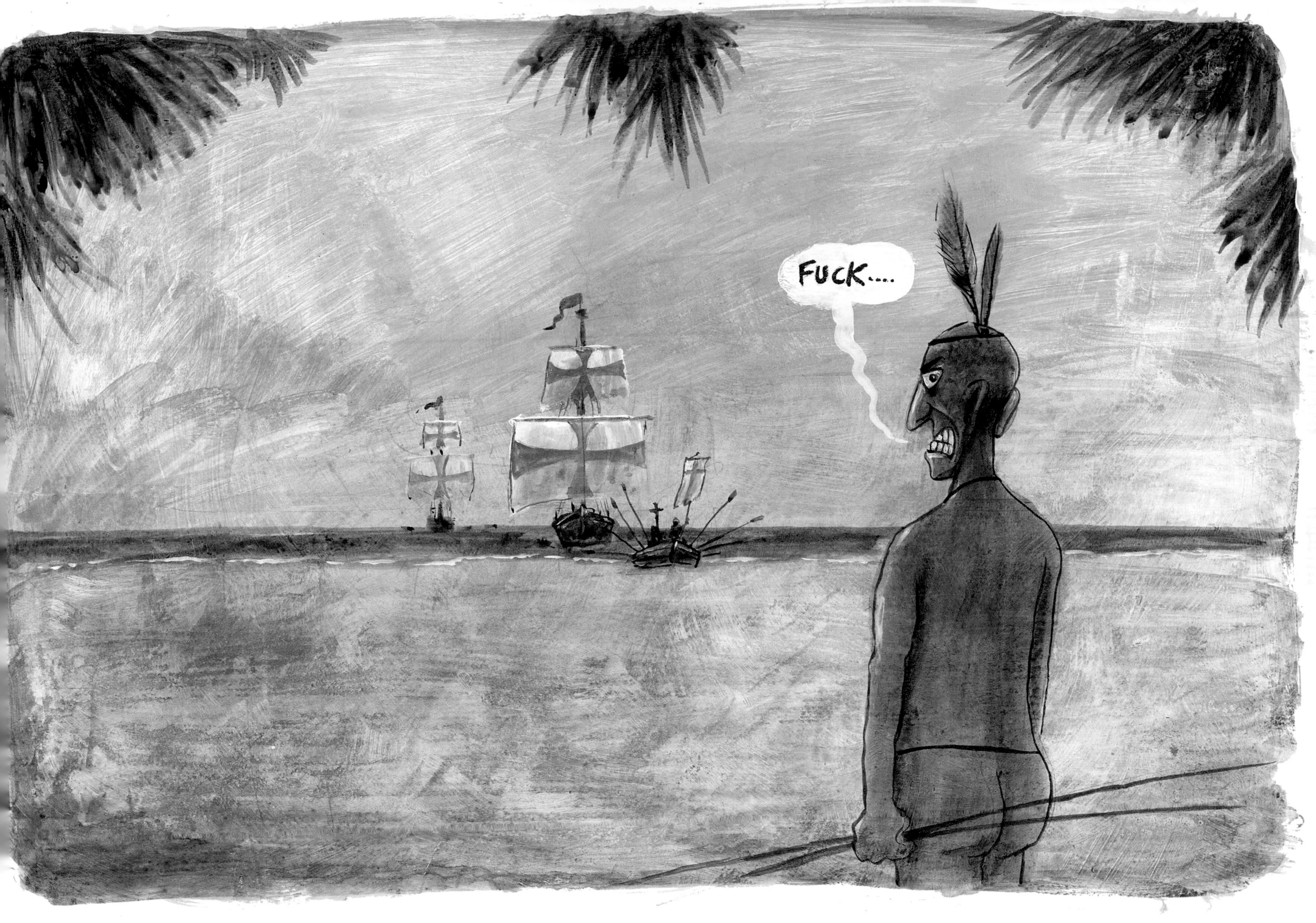
FUCK....

The High Renaissance

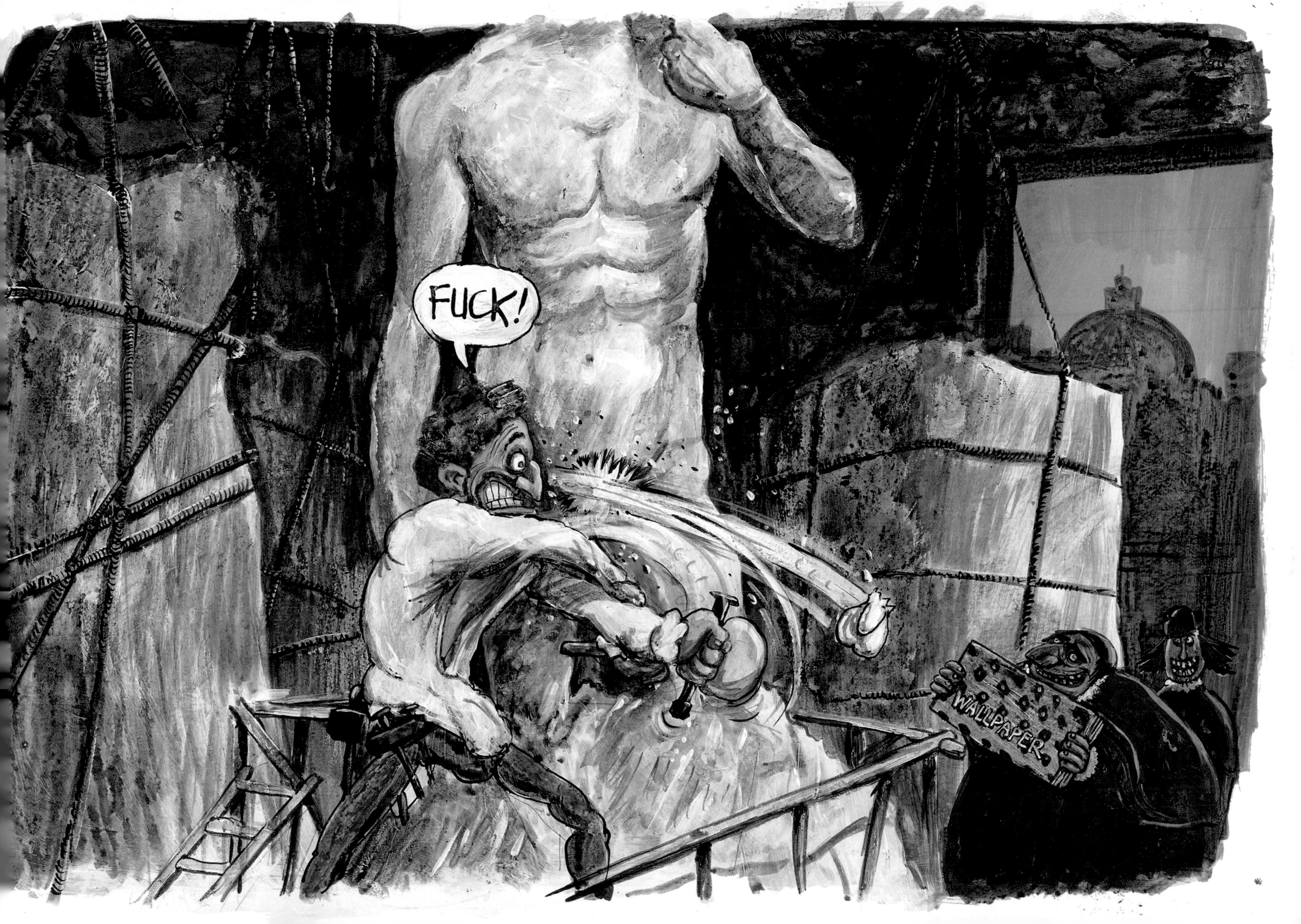
FUCK!
WALLPAPER

Luther Launches the Reformation

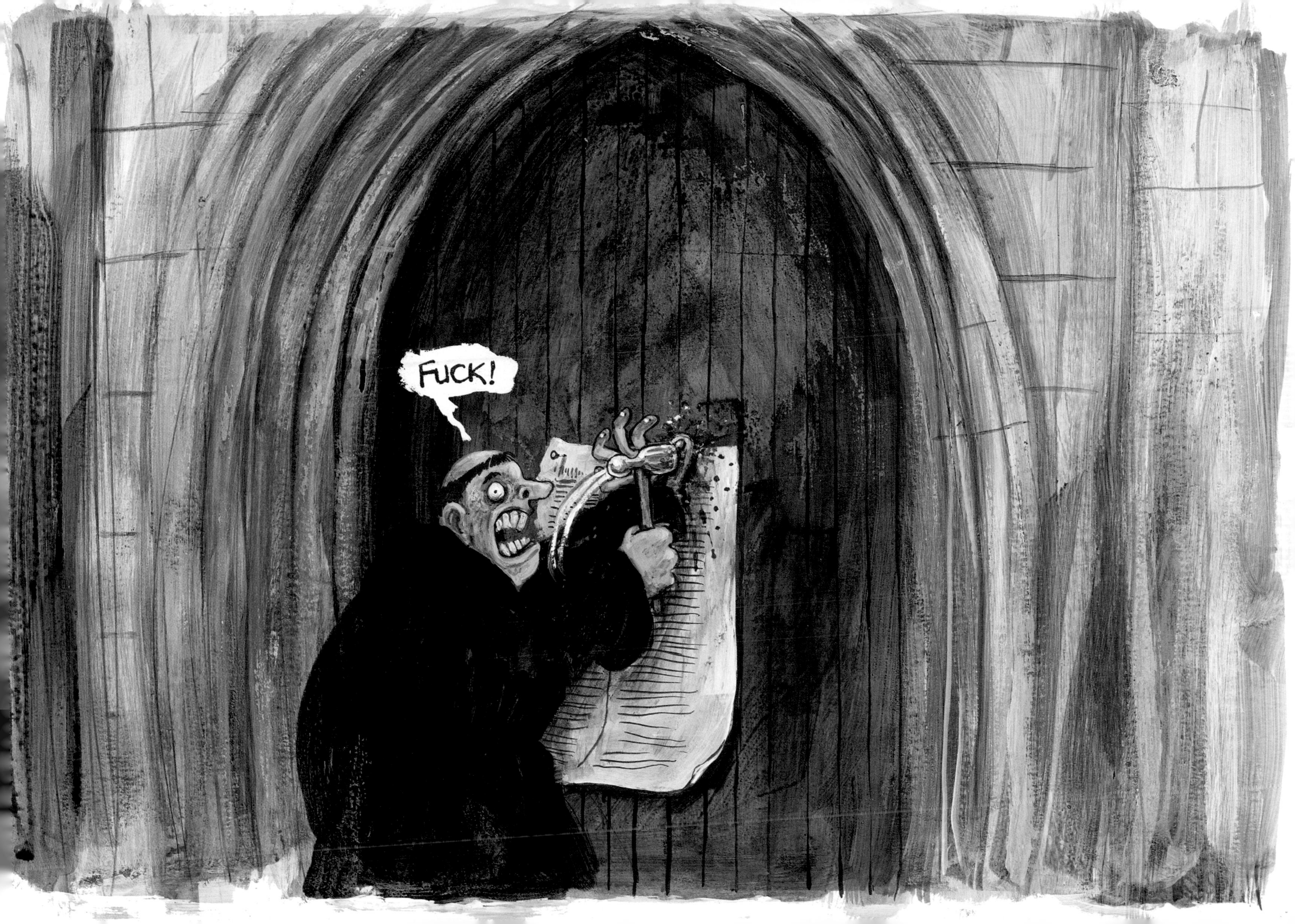
FUCK!

The Shakespearian Theatre

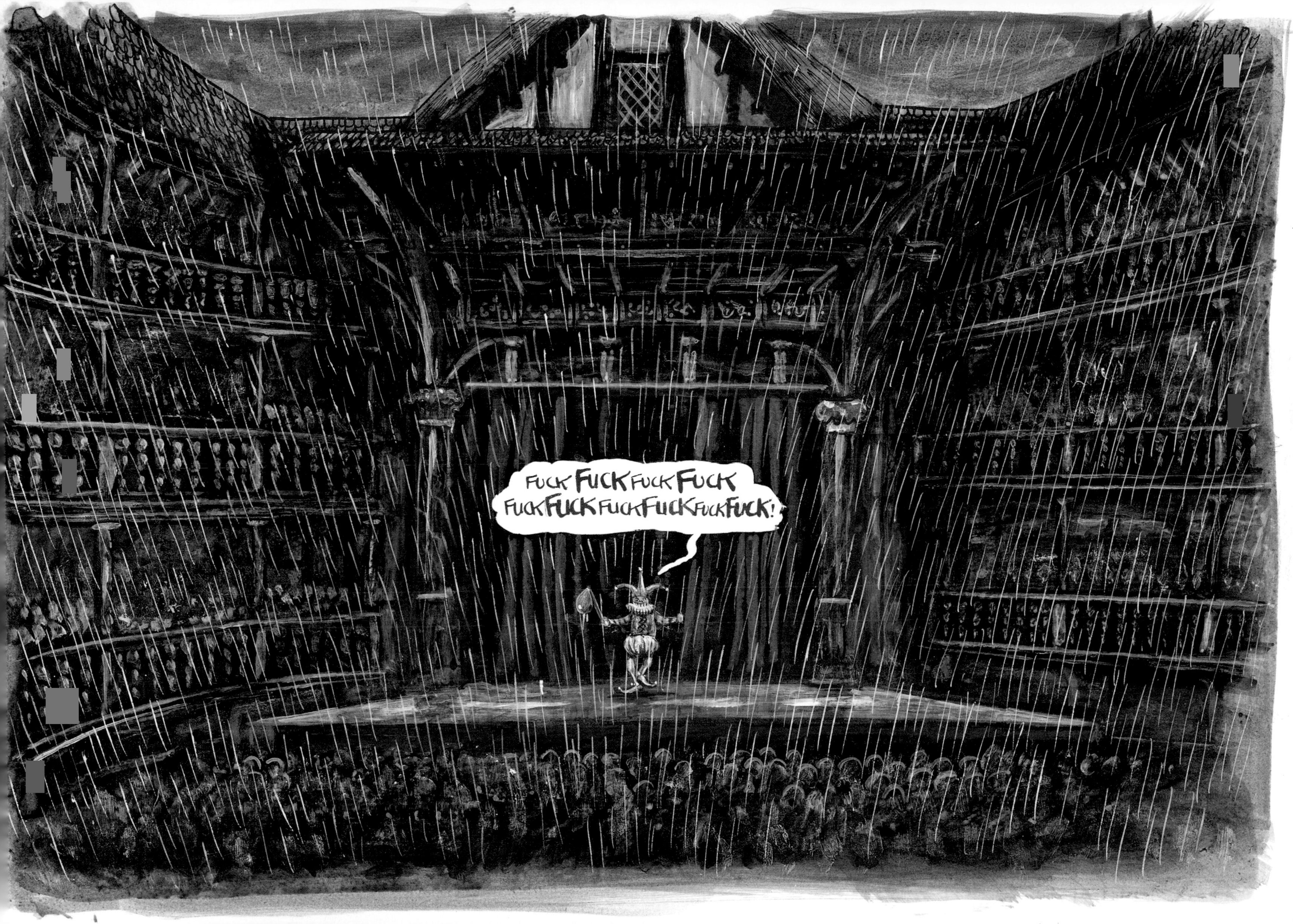
Fuck Fuck Fuck Fuck
Fuck Fuck Fuck Fuck Fuck Fuck!

The English Civil War

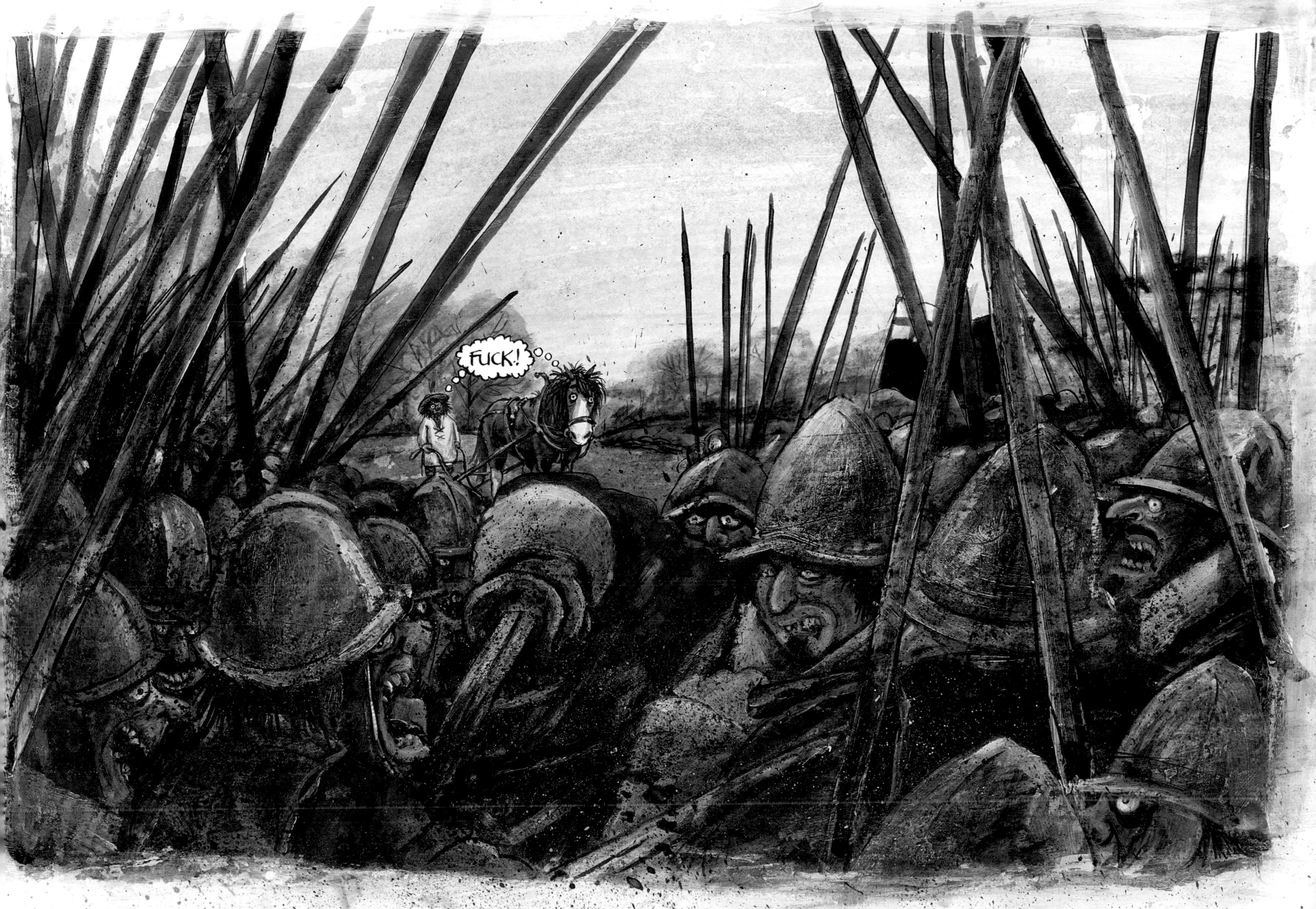
FUCK!

Newton Discovers the Law of Gravity

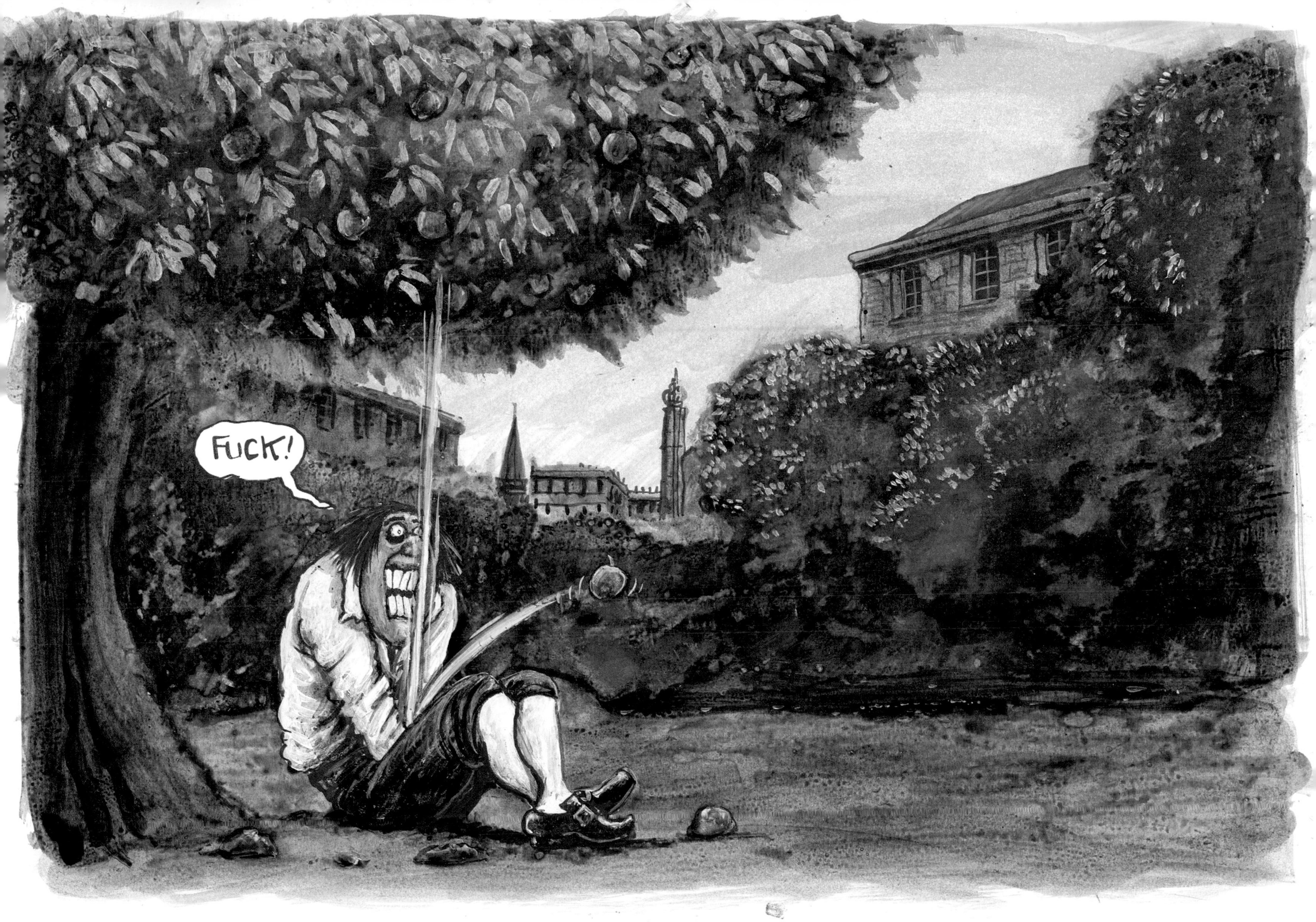
FUCK!

European Absolutism and the Court at Versailles

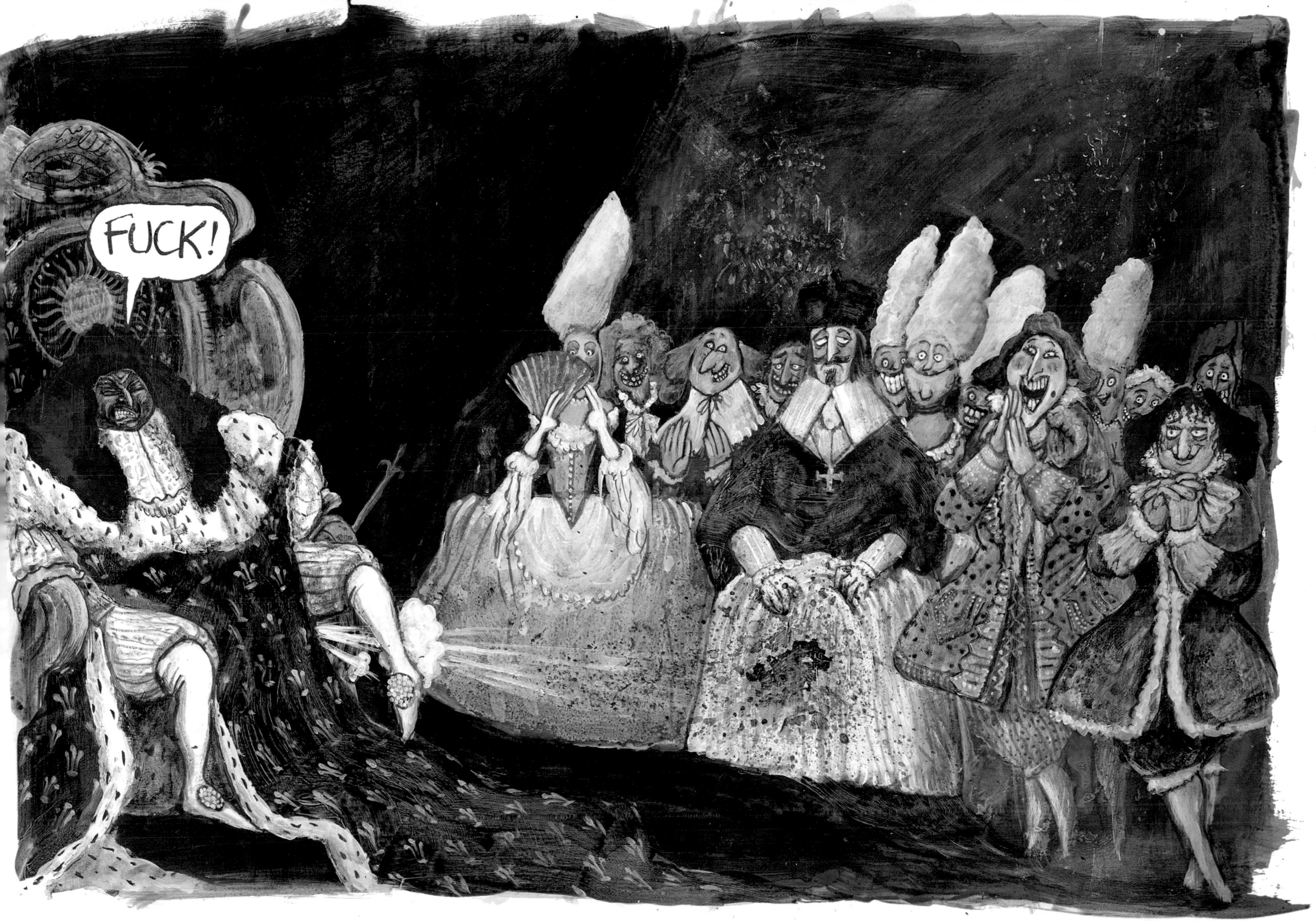
FUCK!

The Age of Reason

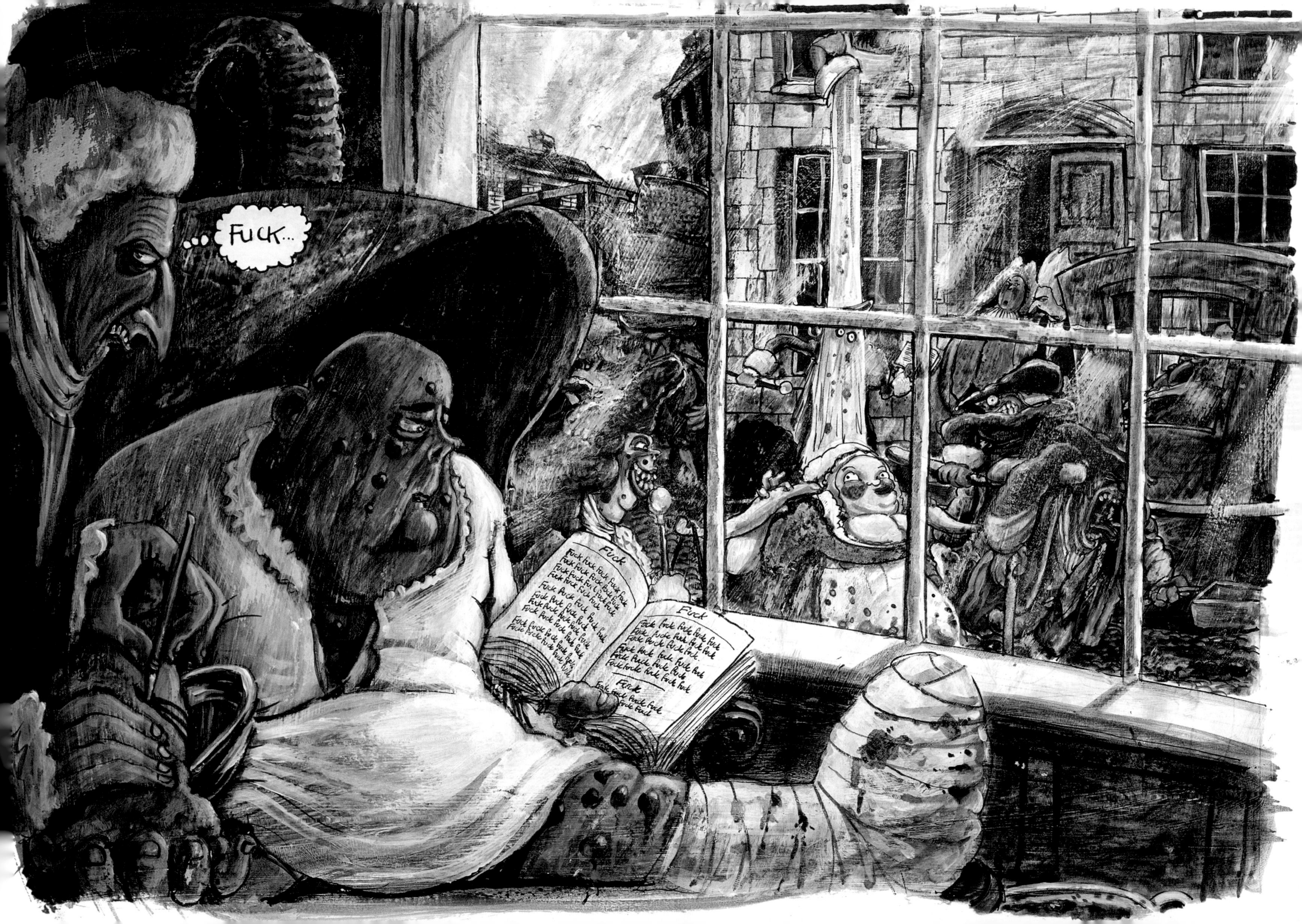

...FUCK...
Fuck
Fuck
Fuck

The Expansion of European Trade

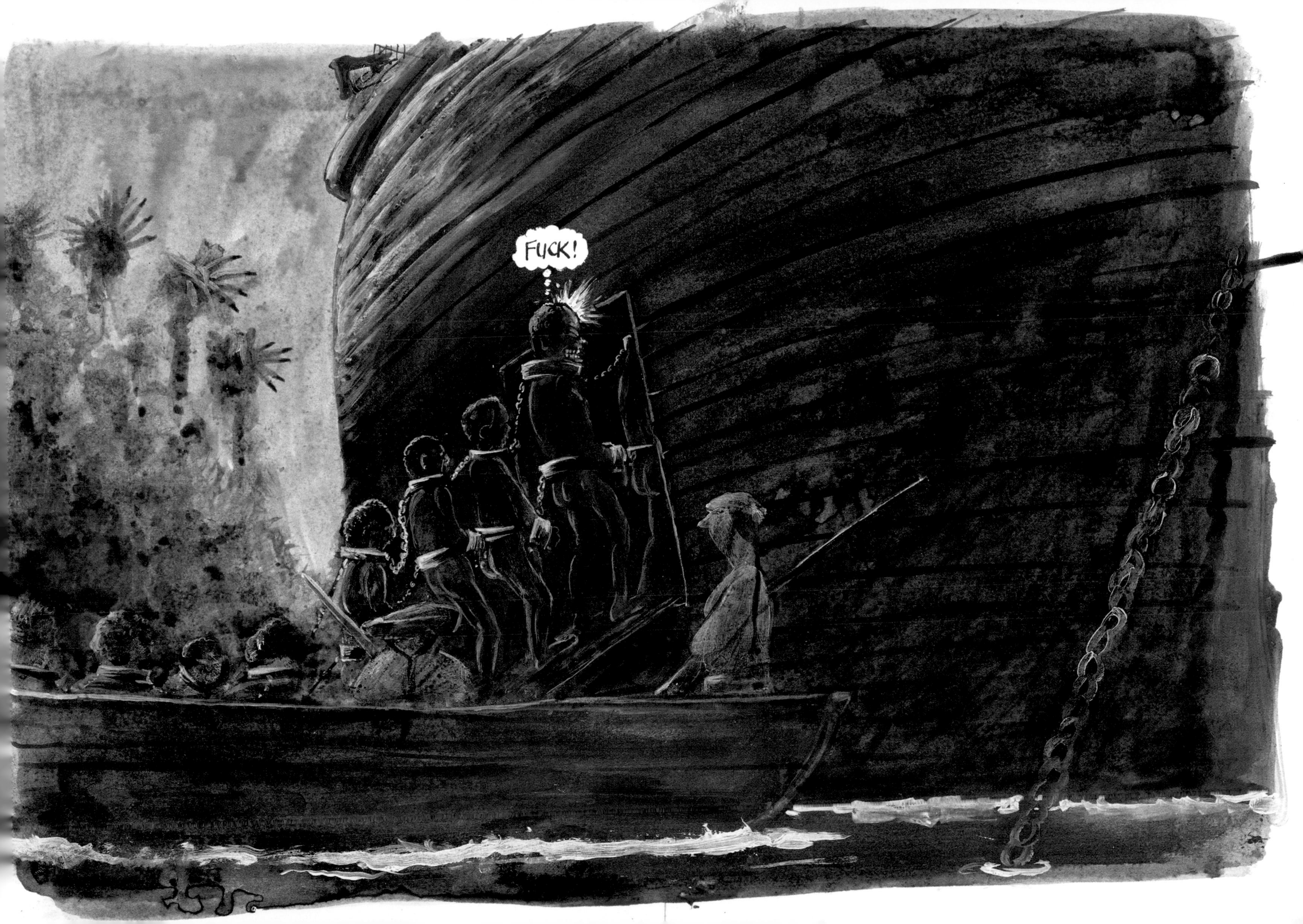
FUCK!

The French Revolution

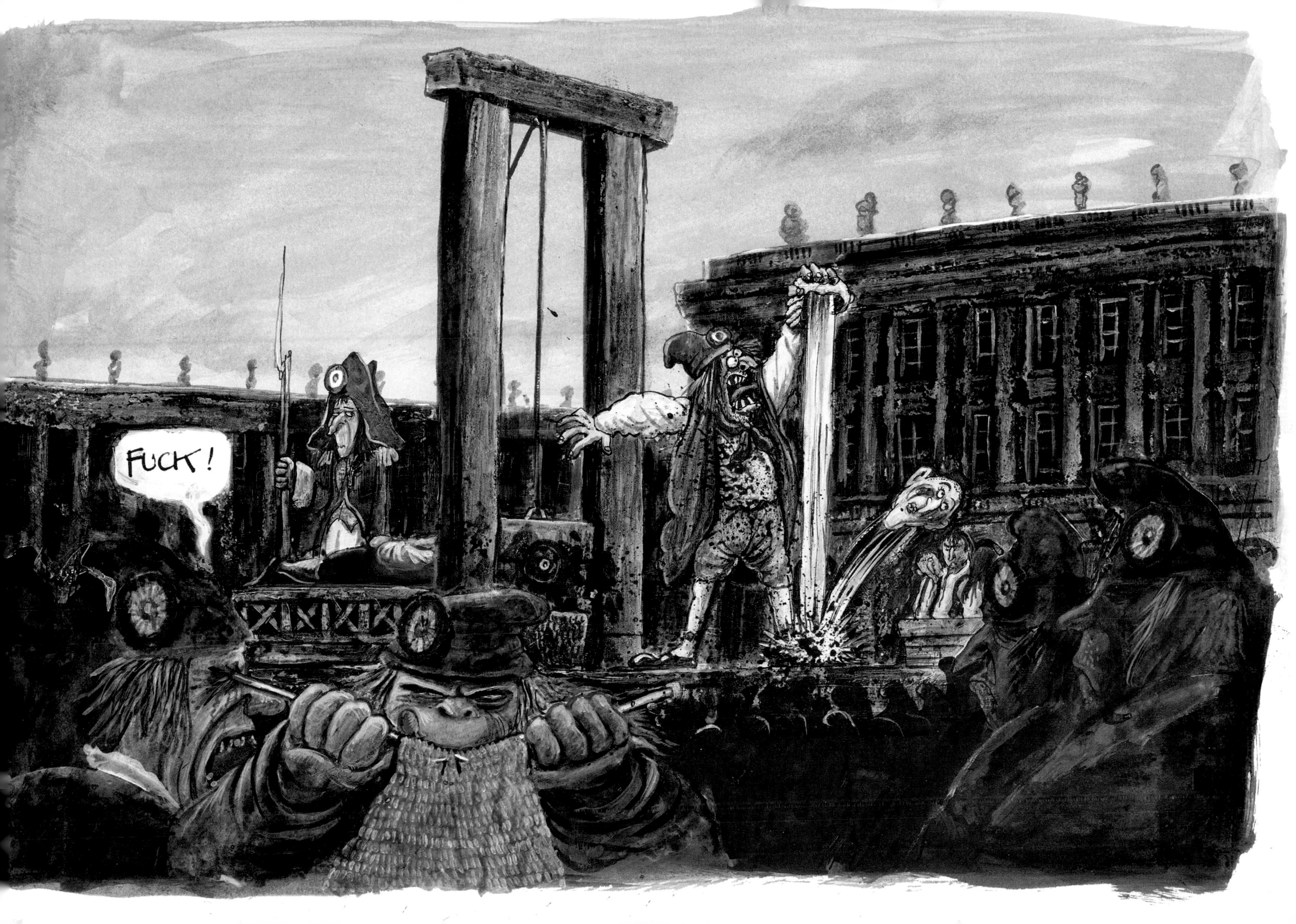
FUCK!

The Romantic Poets

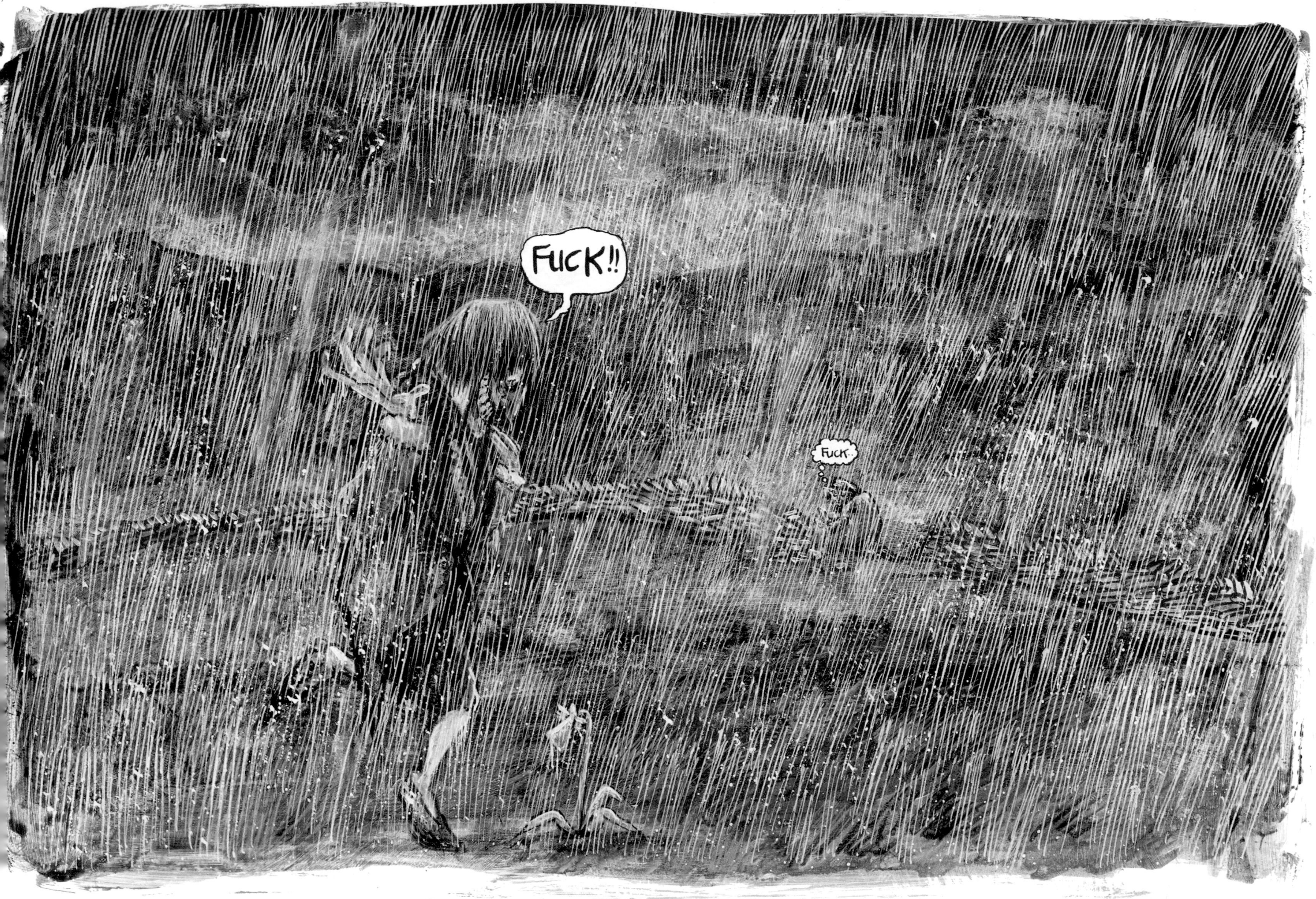
FUCK!!
FUCK..

The Napoleonic Wars

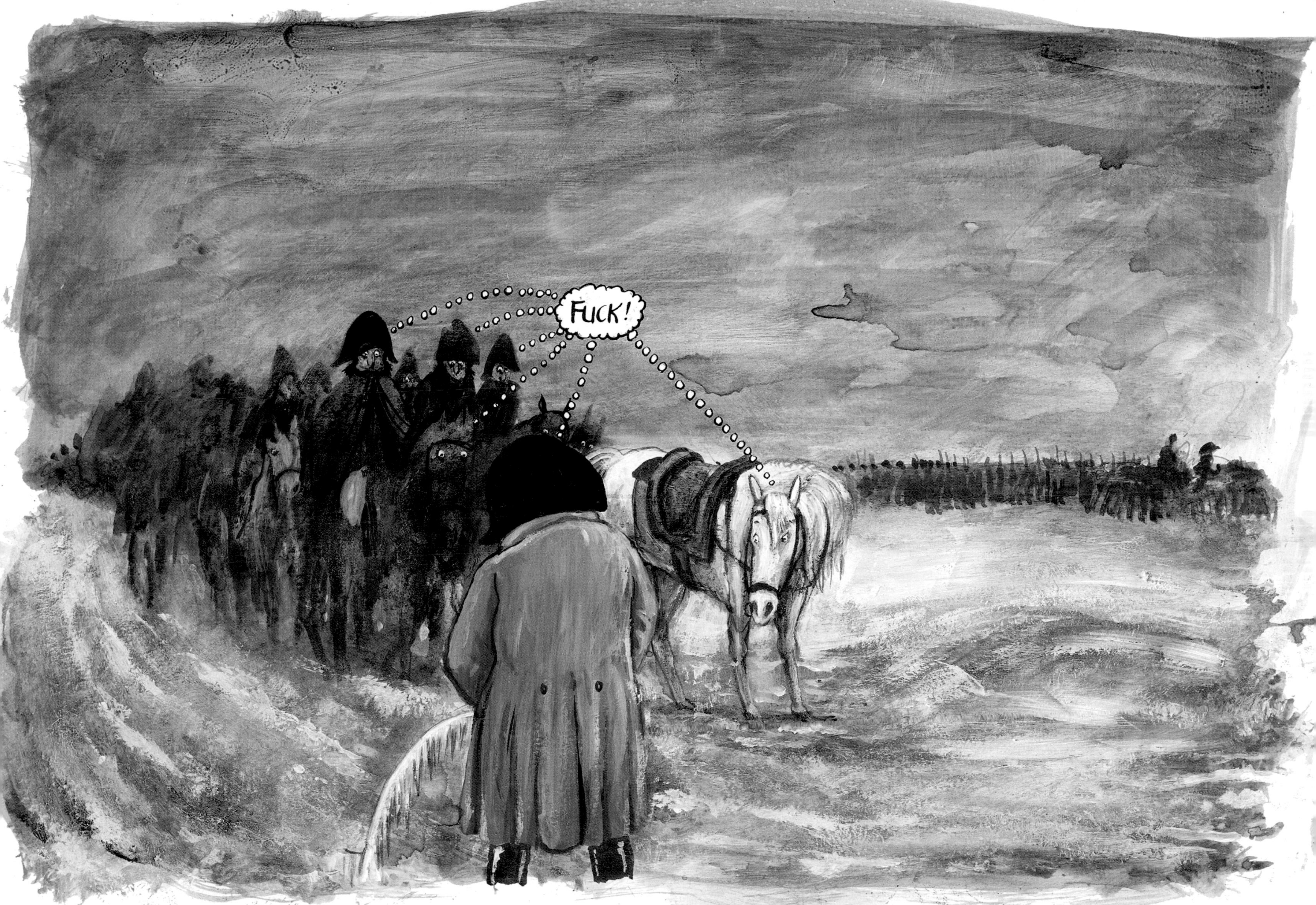
FUCK!

The Industrial Revolution

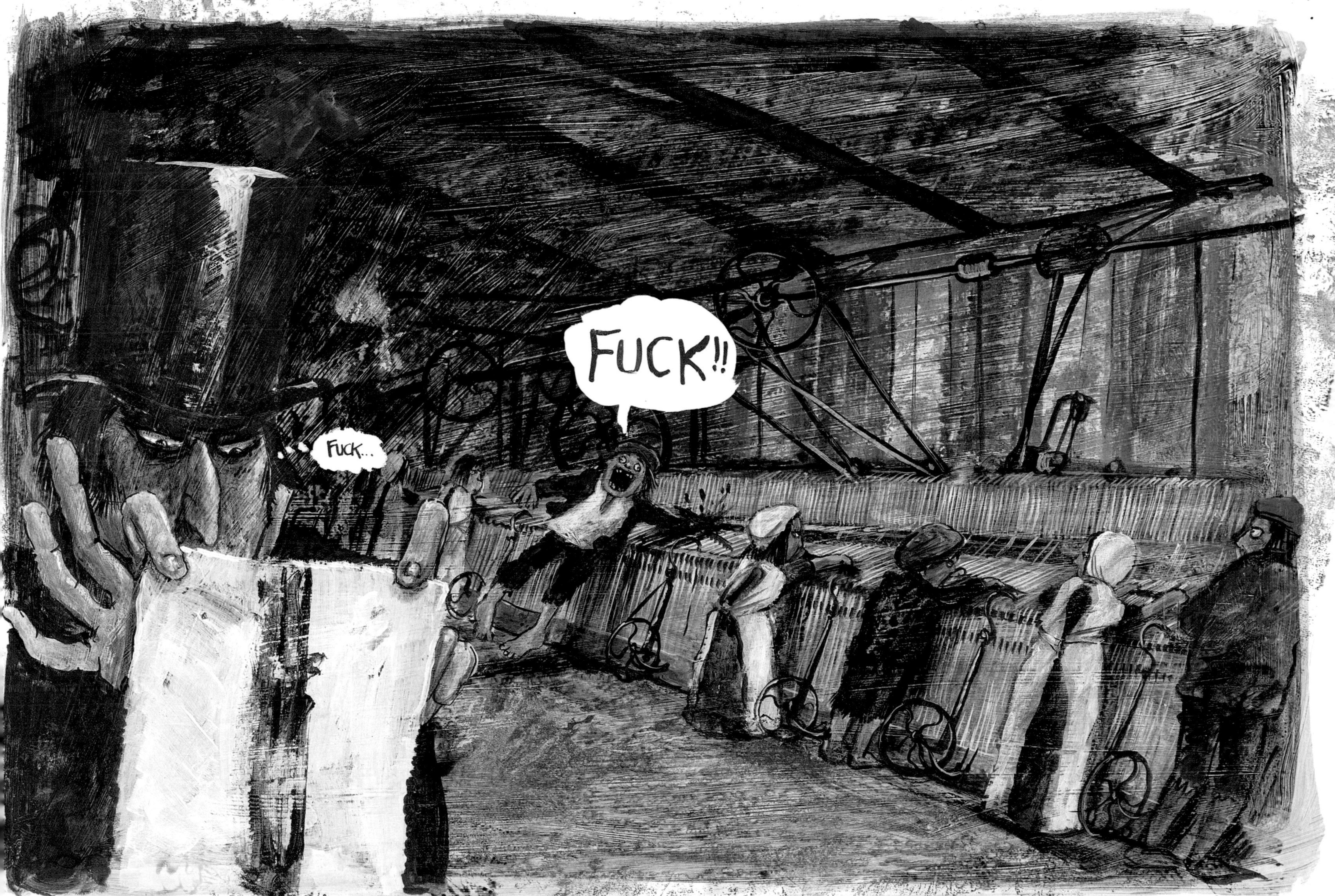
FUCK...
FUCK!!

The British Empire

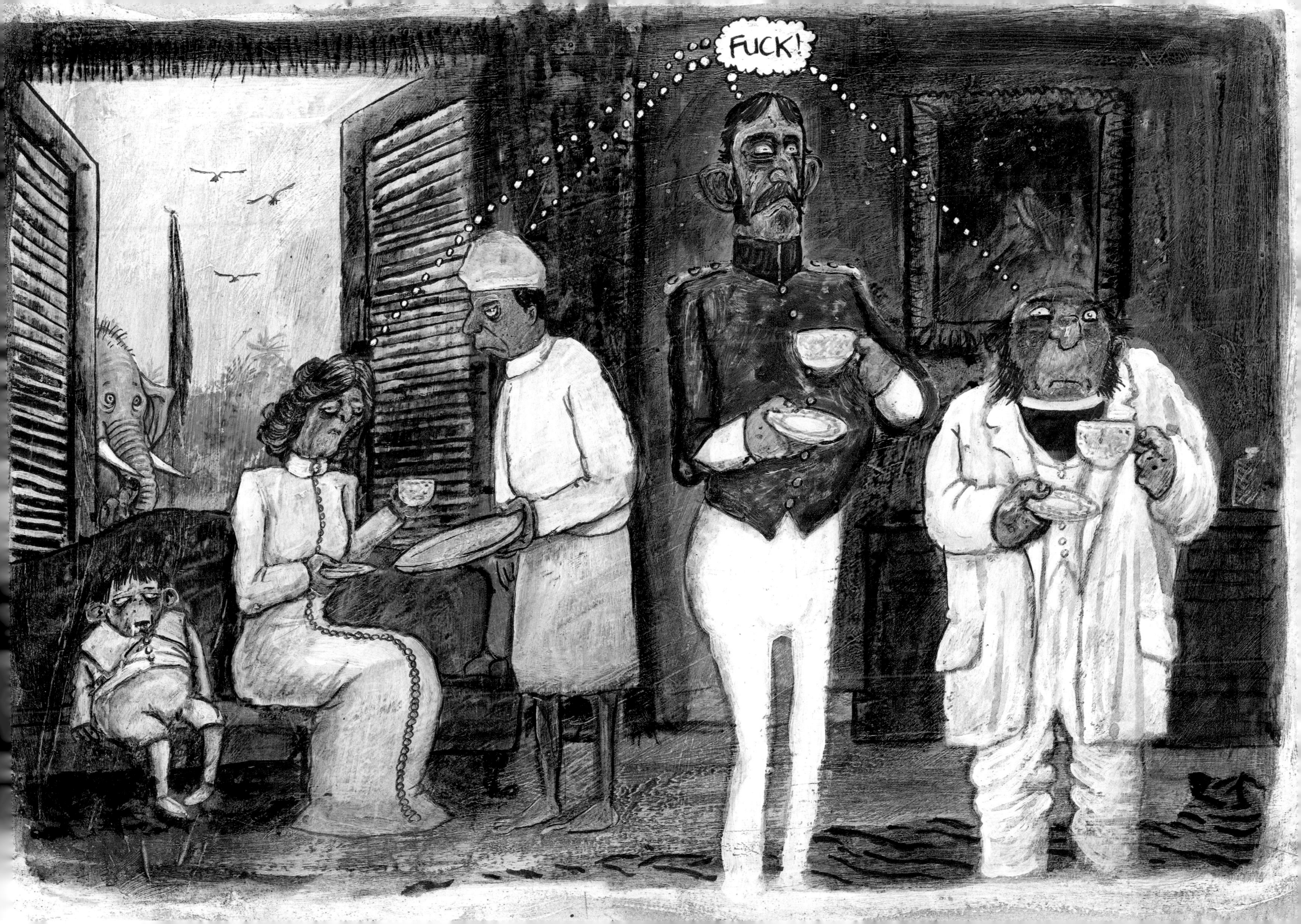
FUCK!

Alexander Graham Bell Invents the Telephone

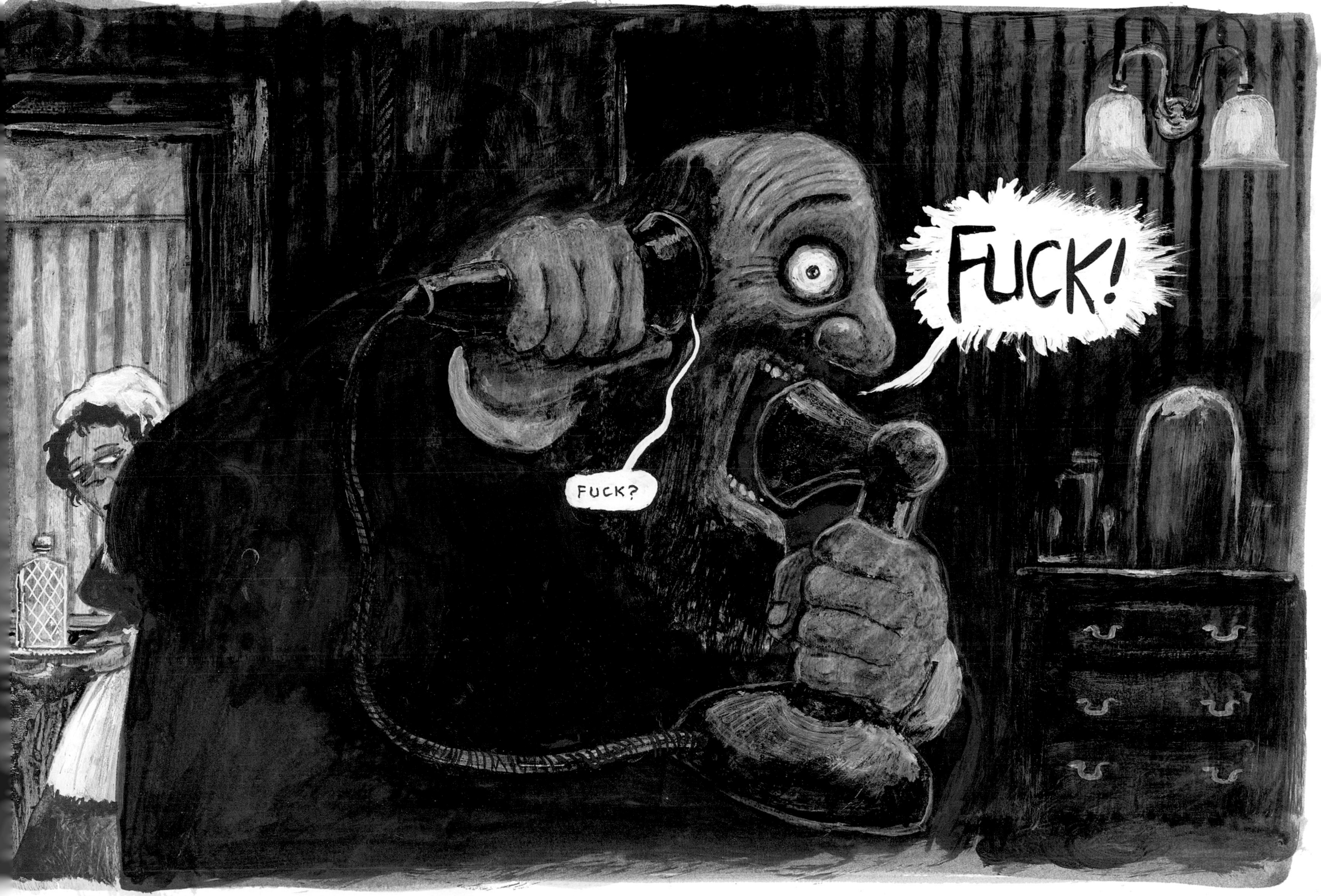
FUCK!
FUCK?

The Impressionists

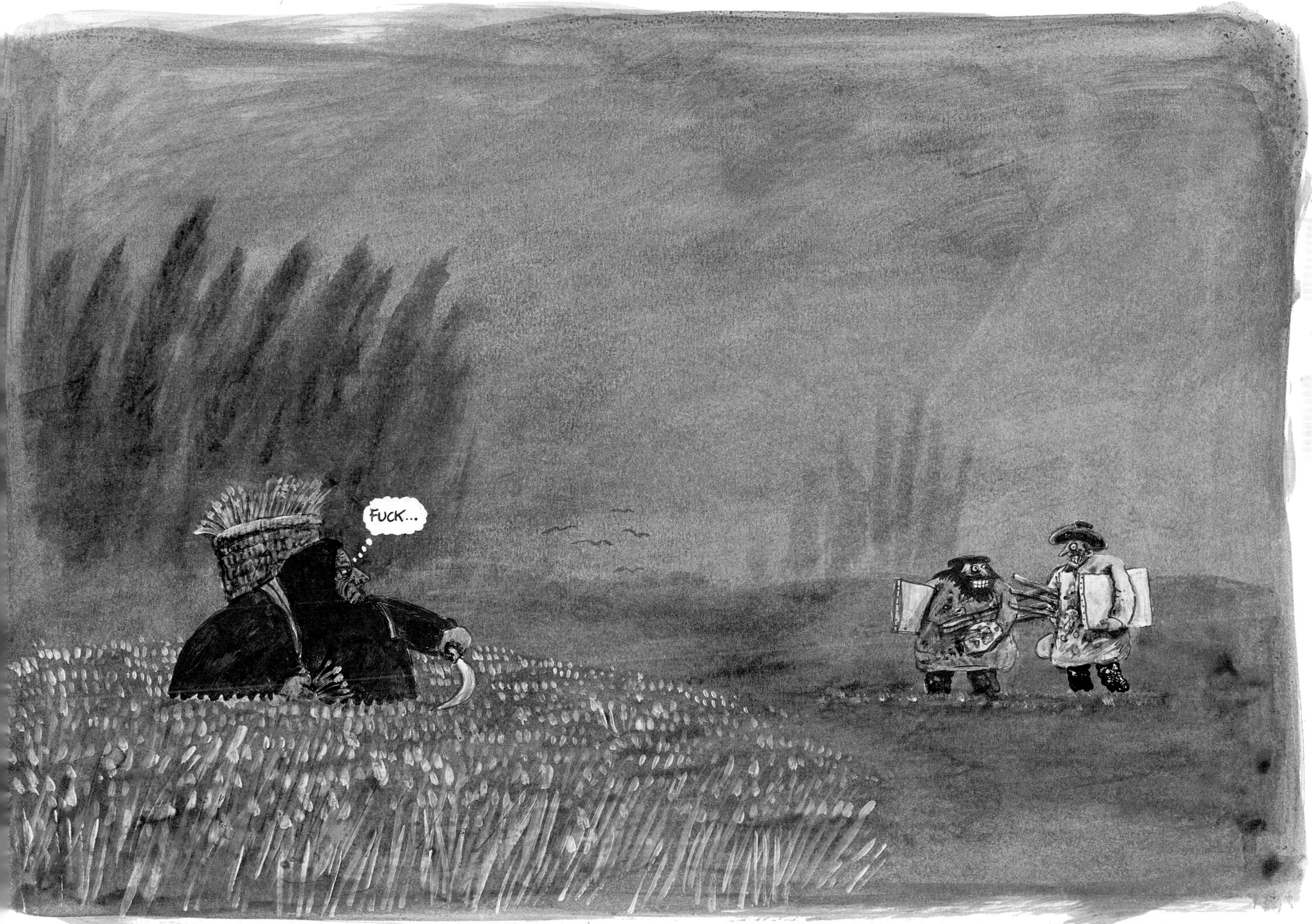
FUCK...

London: The Capital of Empire

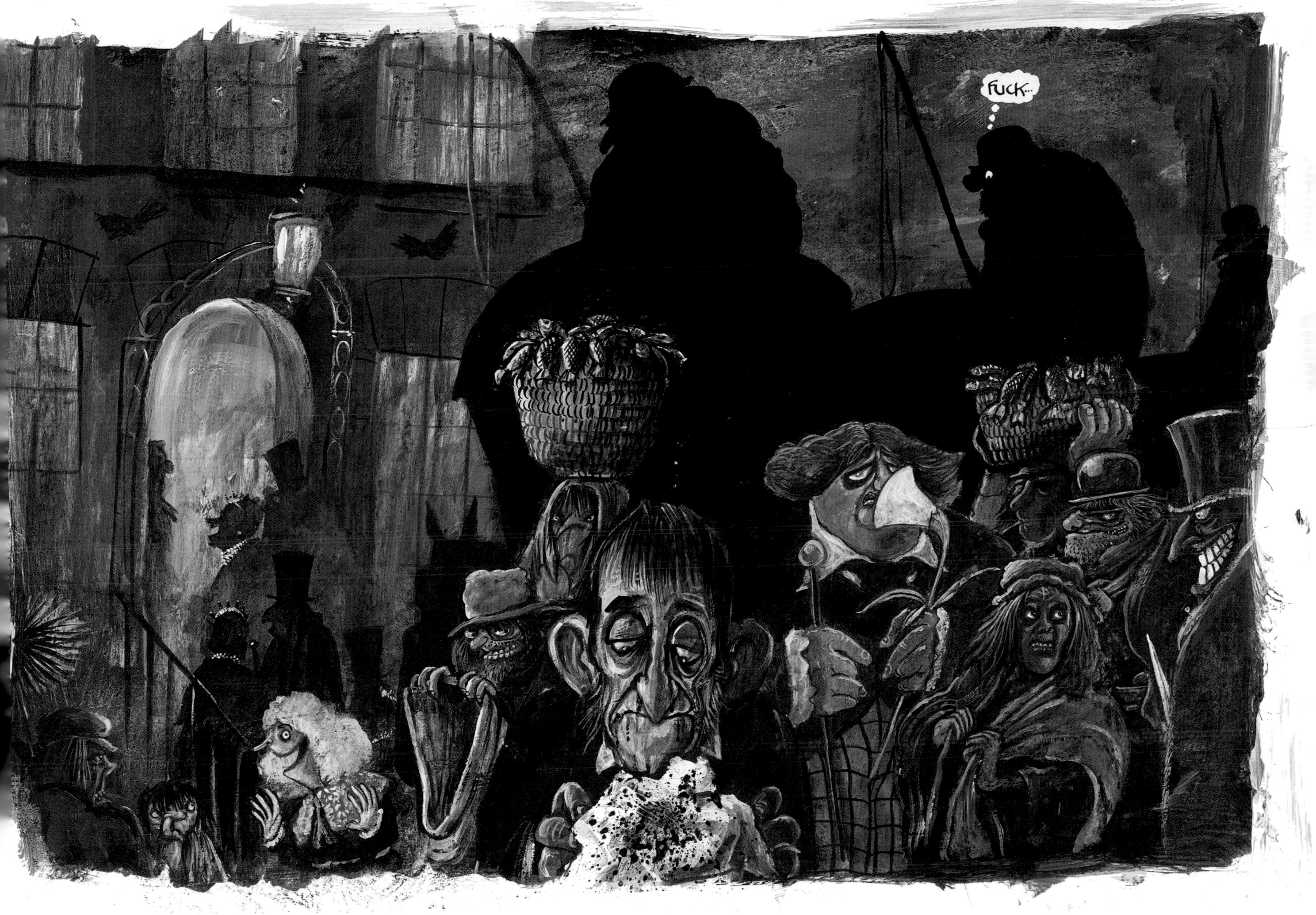
FUCK...

Freud Unlocks the Secrets of the Mind

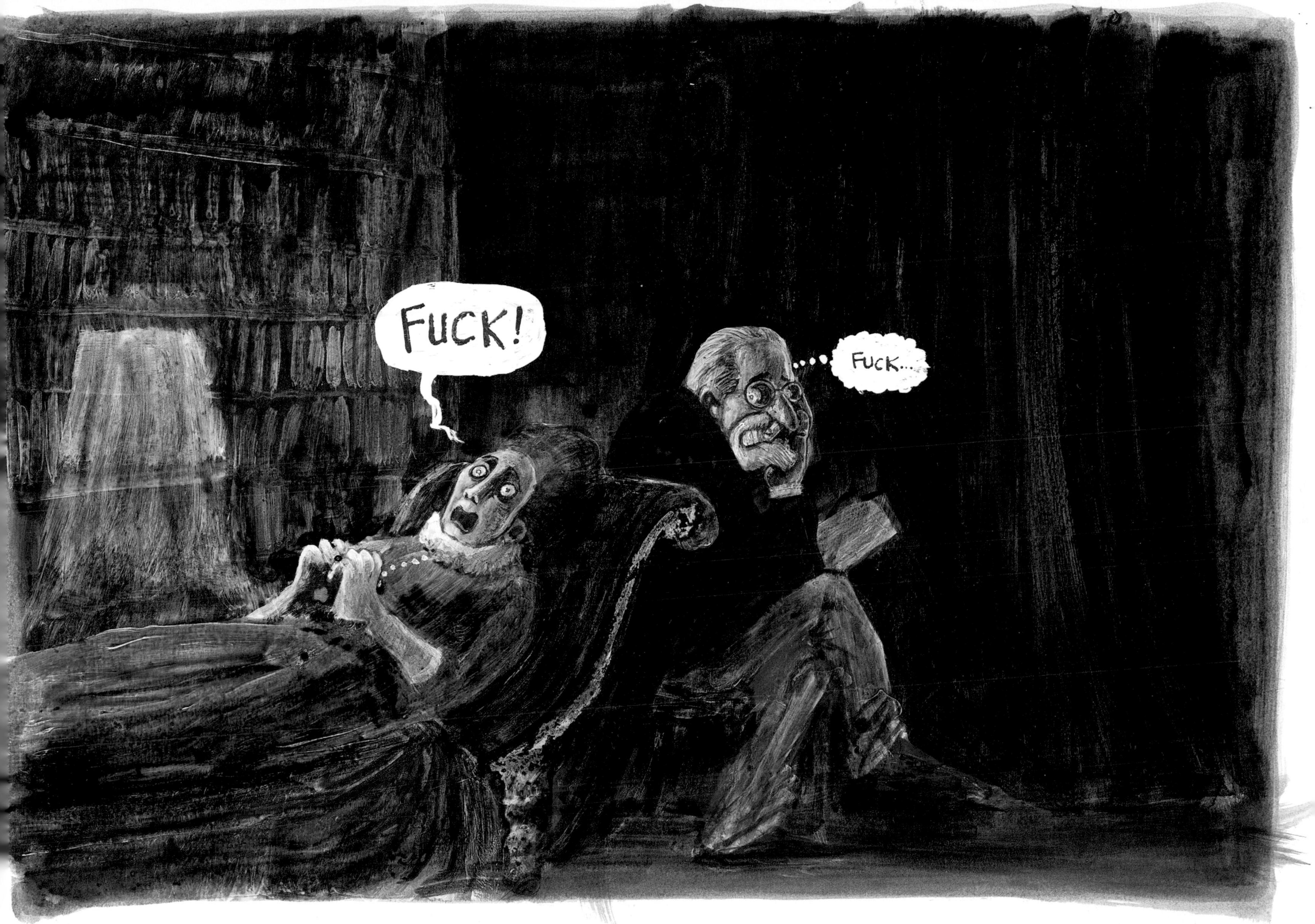
FUCK!
FUCK...

The Wright Brothers Conquer the Air

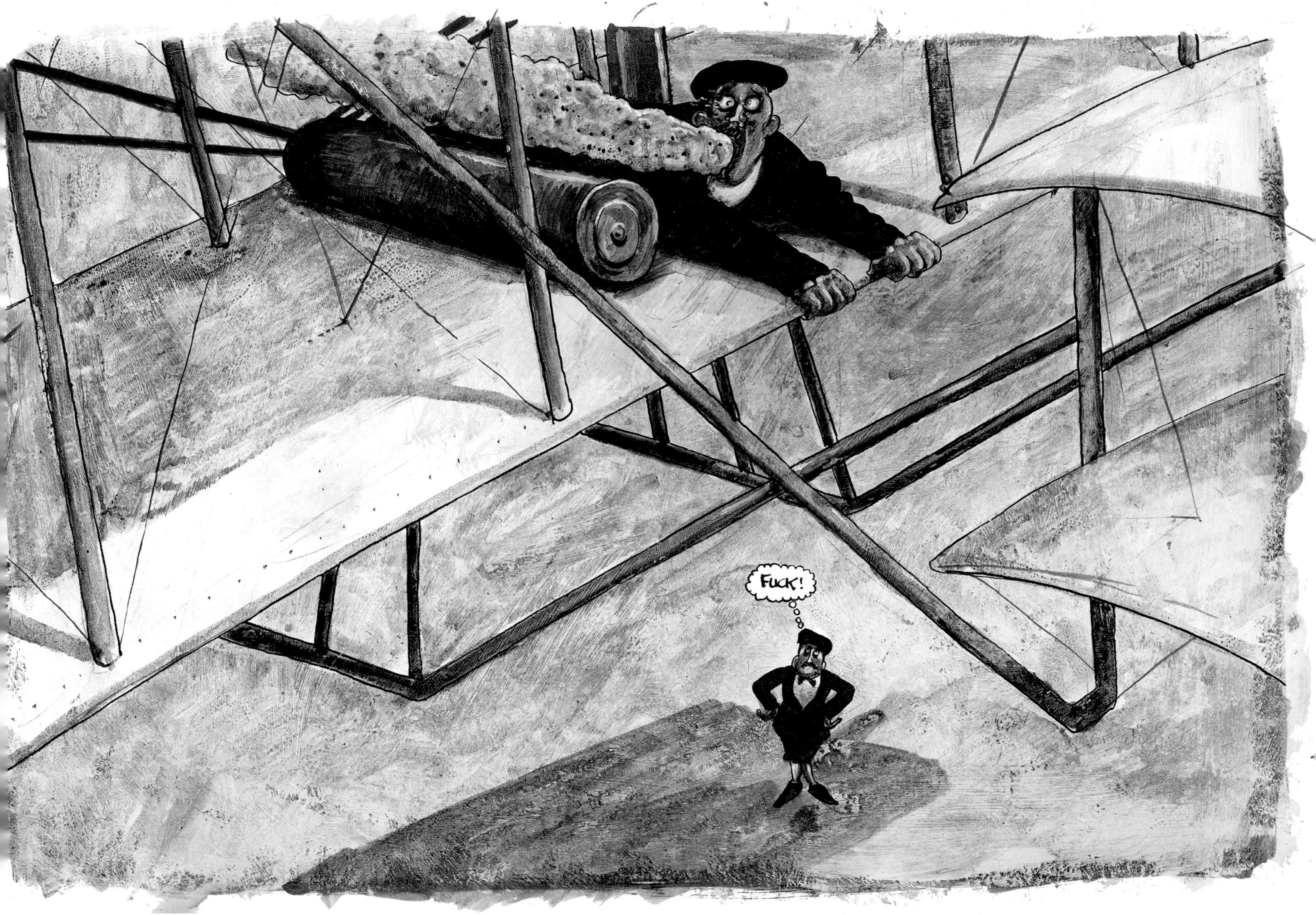
FUCK!

Oates Leaves Captain Scott's Tent

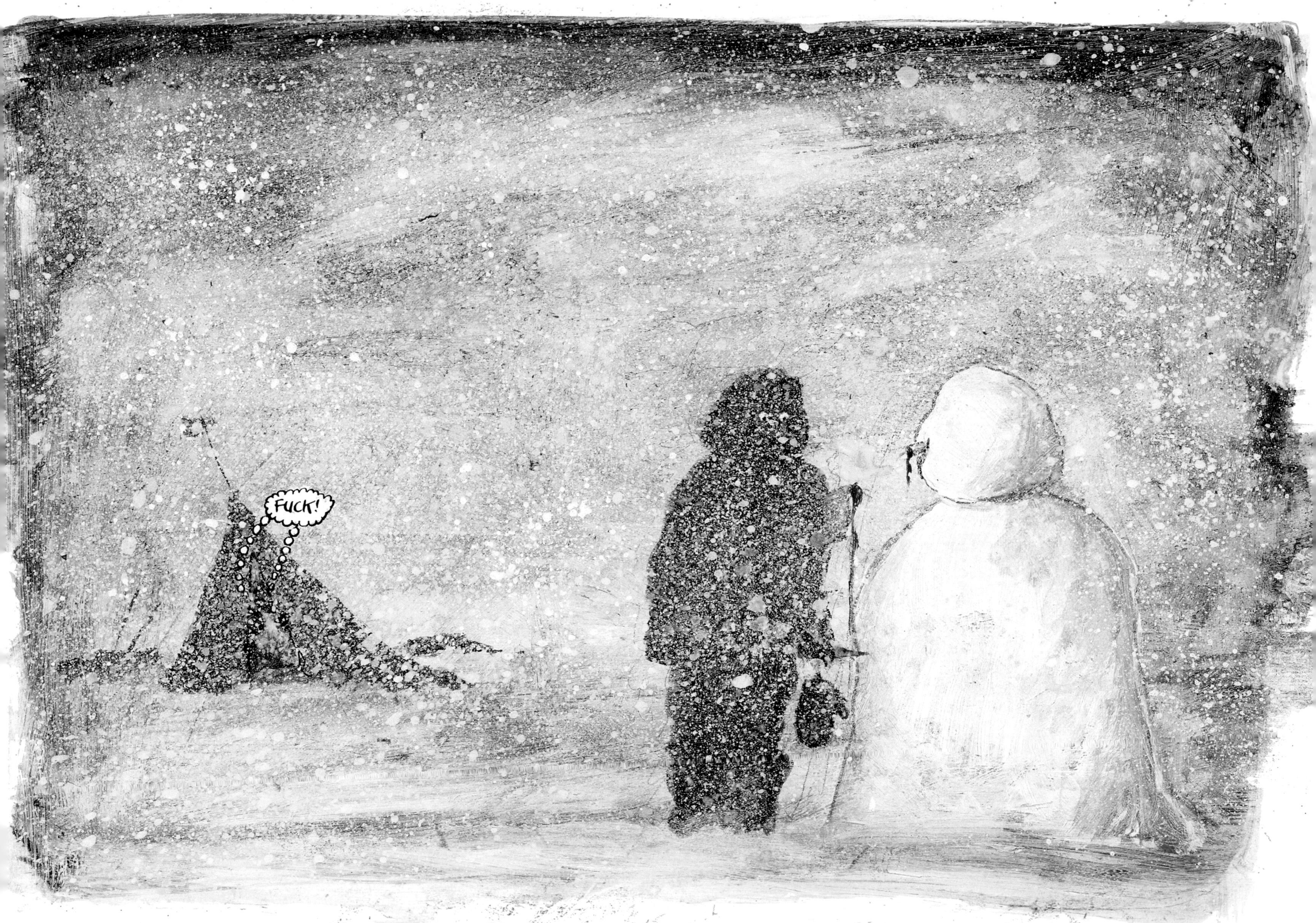
FUCK!

The Great War

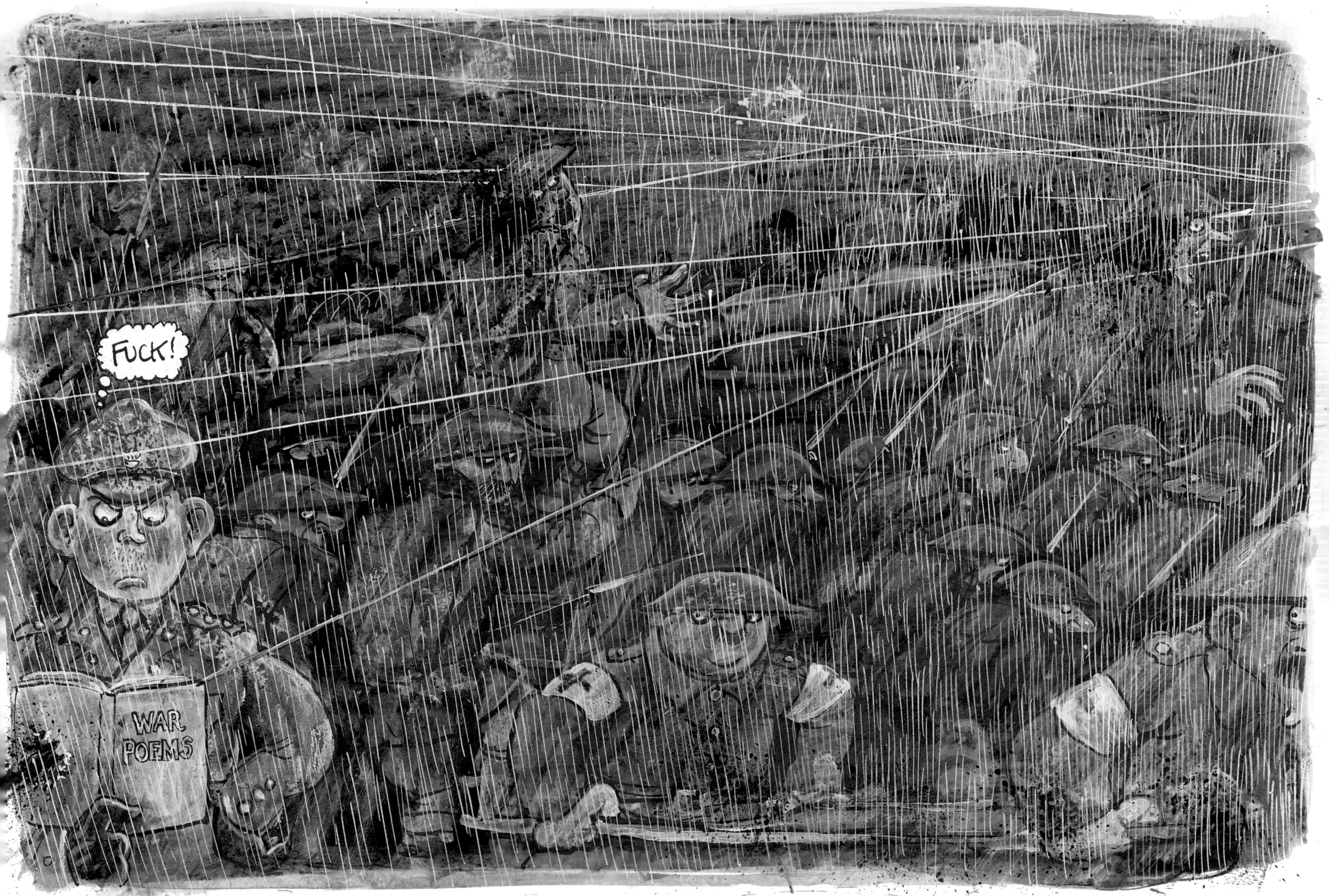
FUCK!
WAR POEMS

The Great Depression

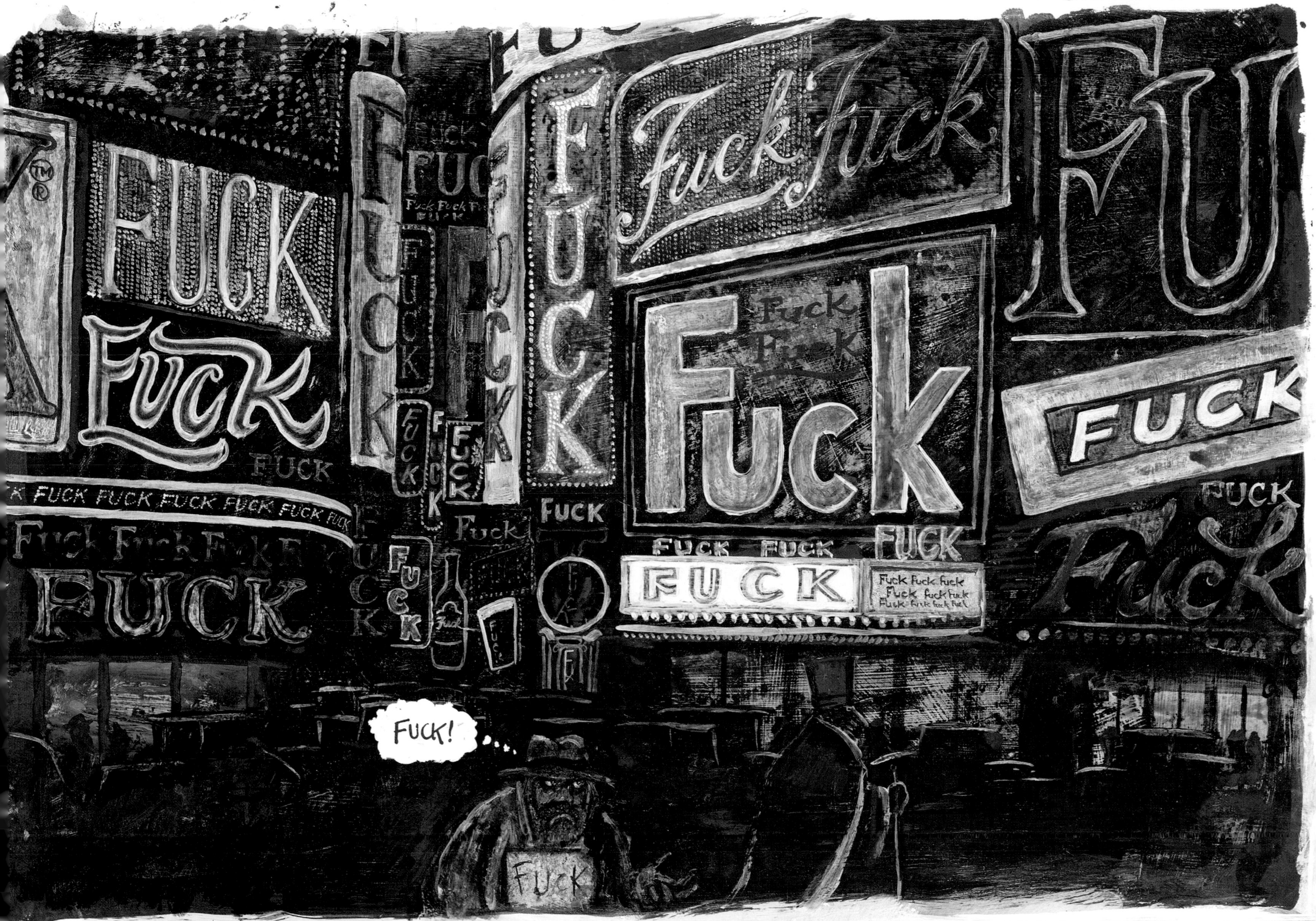
FUCK
FUCK
FUCK
FUCK
FUCK FUCK FUCK FUCK FUCK FUCK
FUCK
Fuck Fuck
FUCK
FUCK
Fuck Fuck
Fuck
FUCK FUCK FUCK
FUCK
Fuck fuck fuck
Fuck fuck fuck
FUCK
FUCK
FUCK!
FUCK

Man's Inhumanity to Man

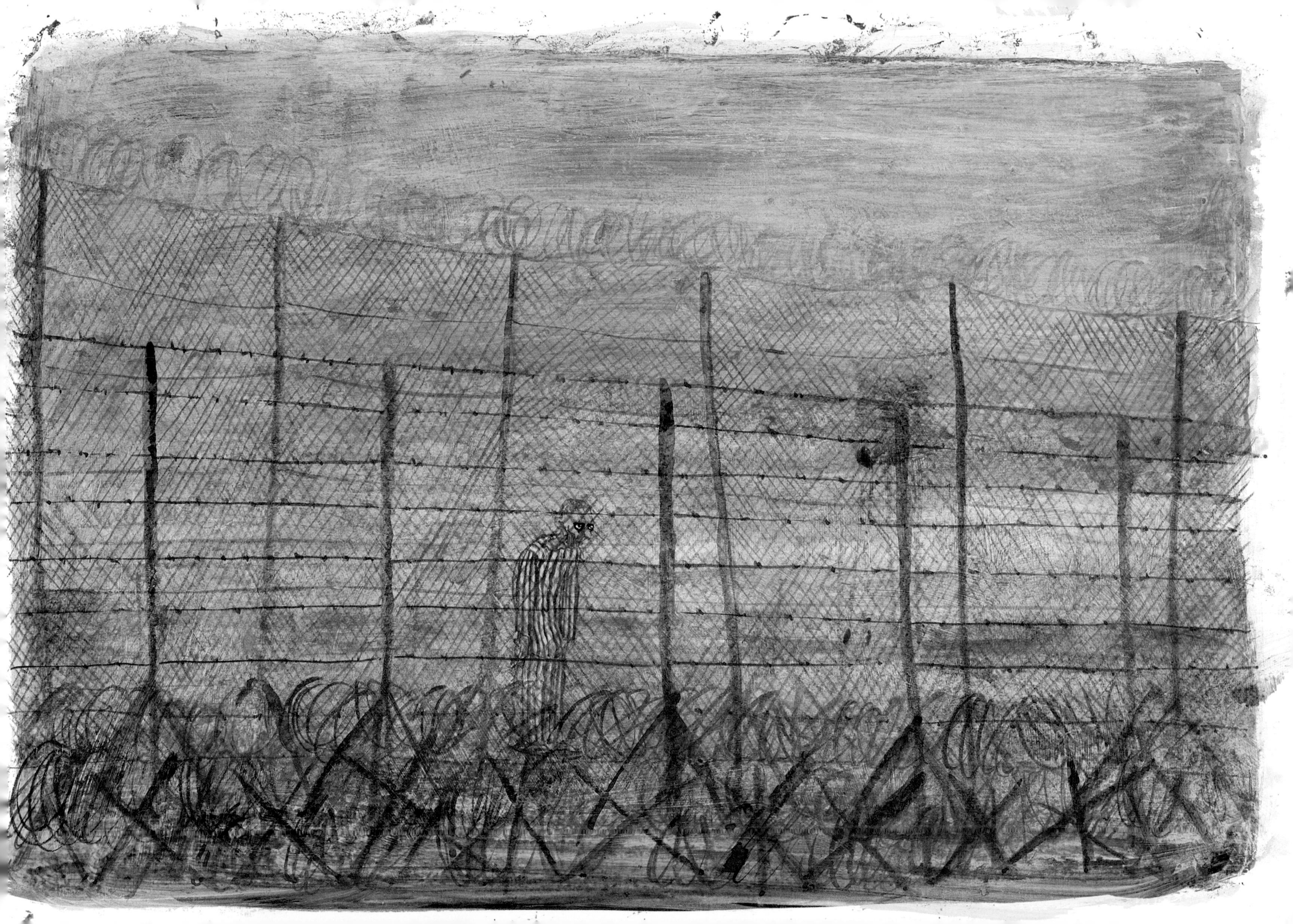

Man Harnesses the Power of the Atom

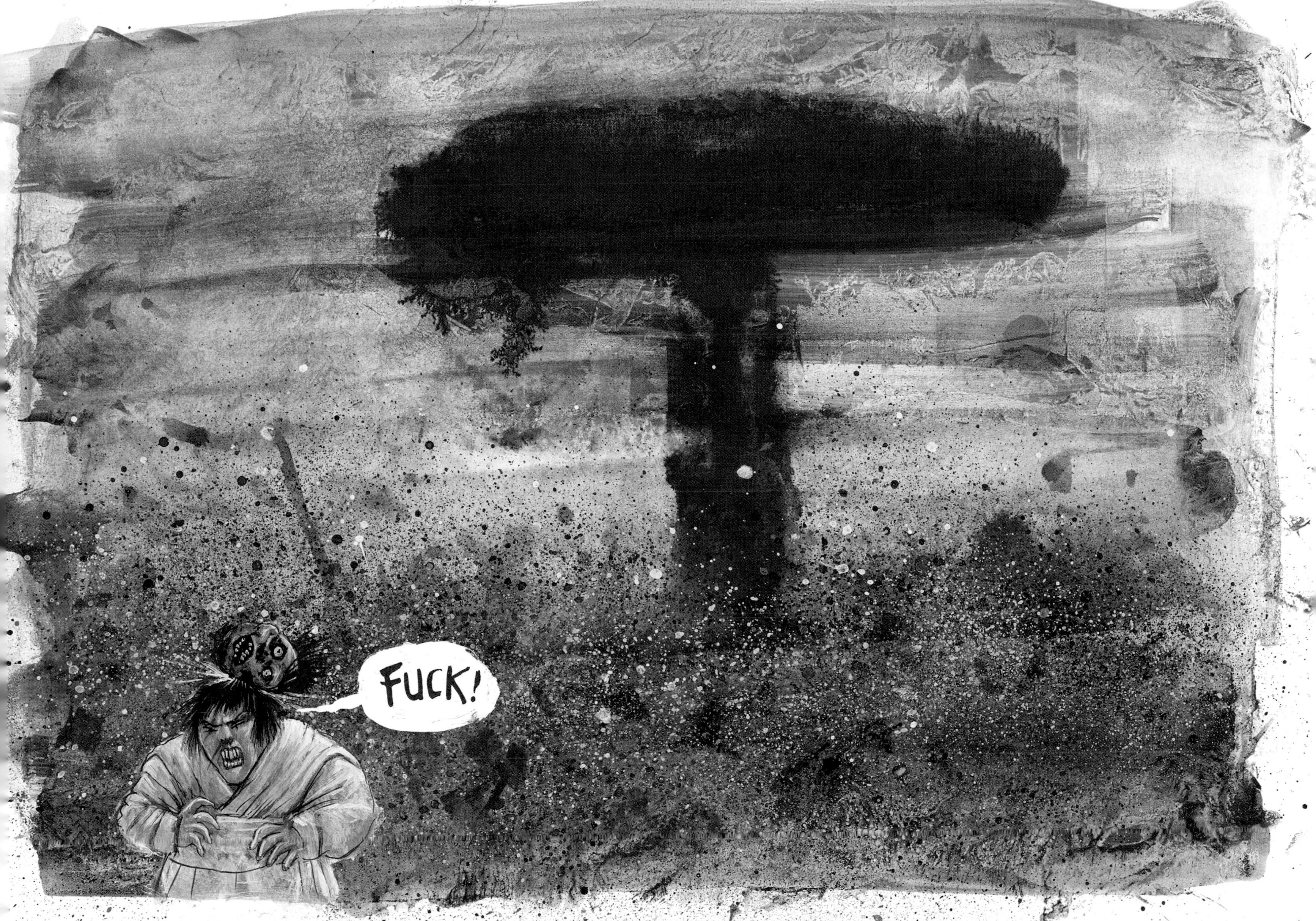
FUCK!

The Great Society

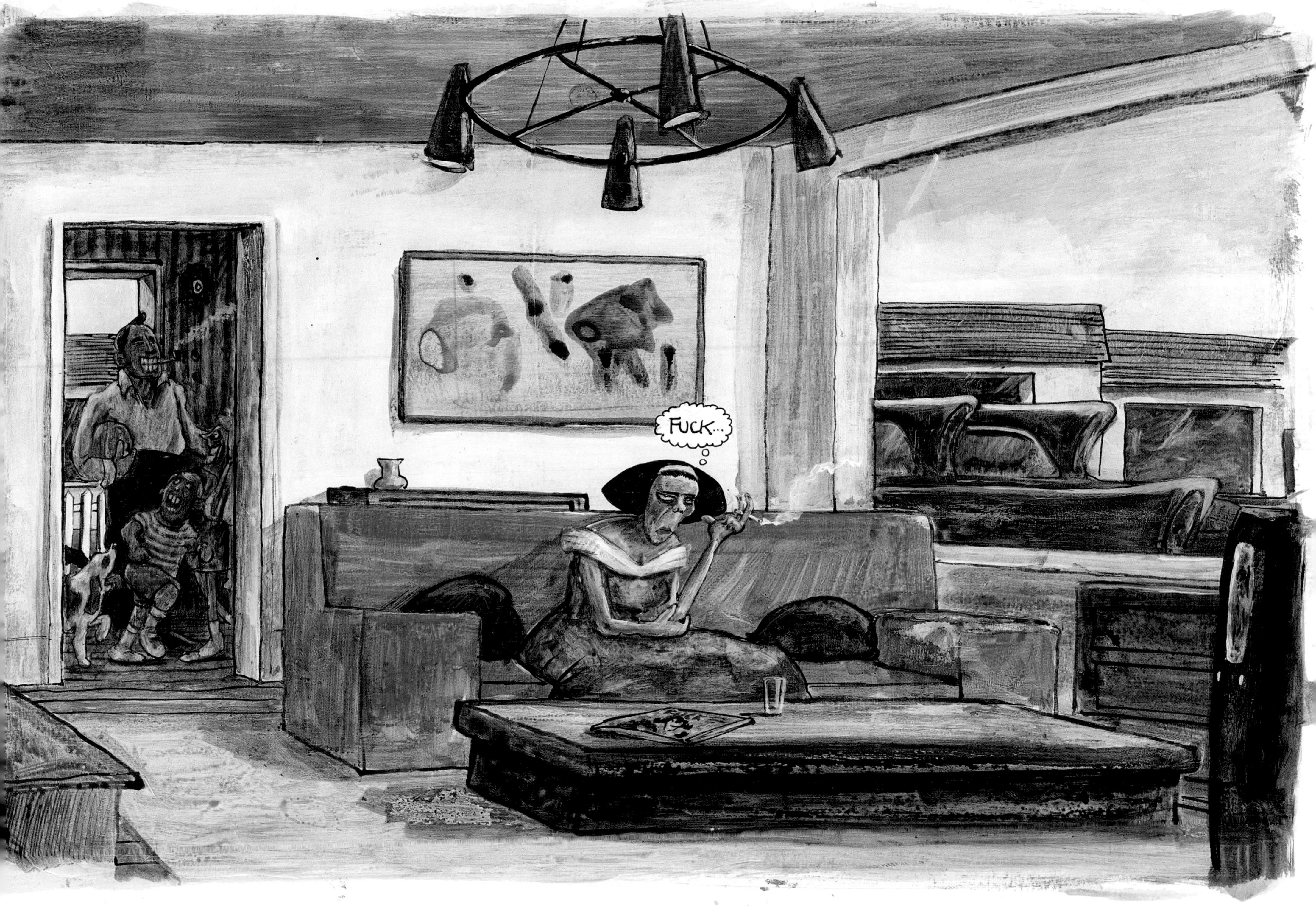
FUCK...

The Consumer Revolution

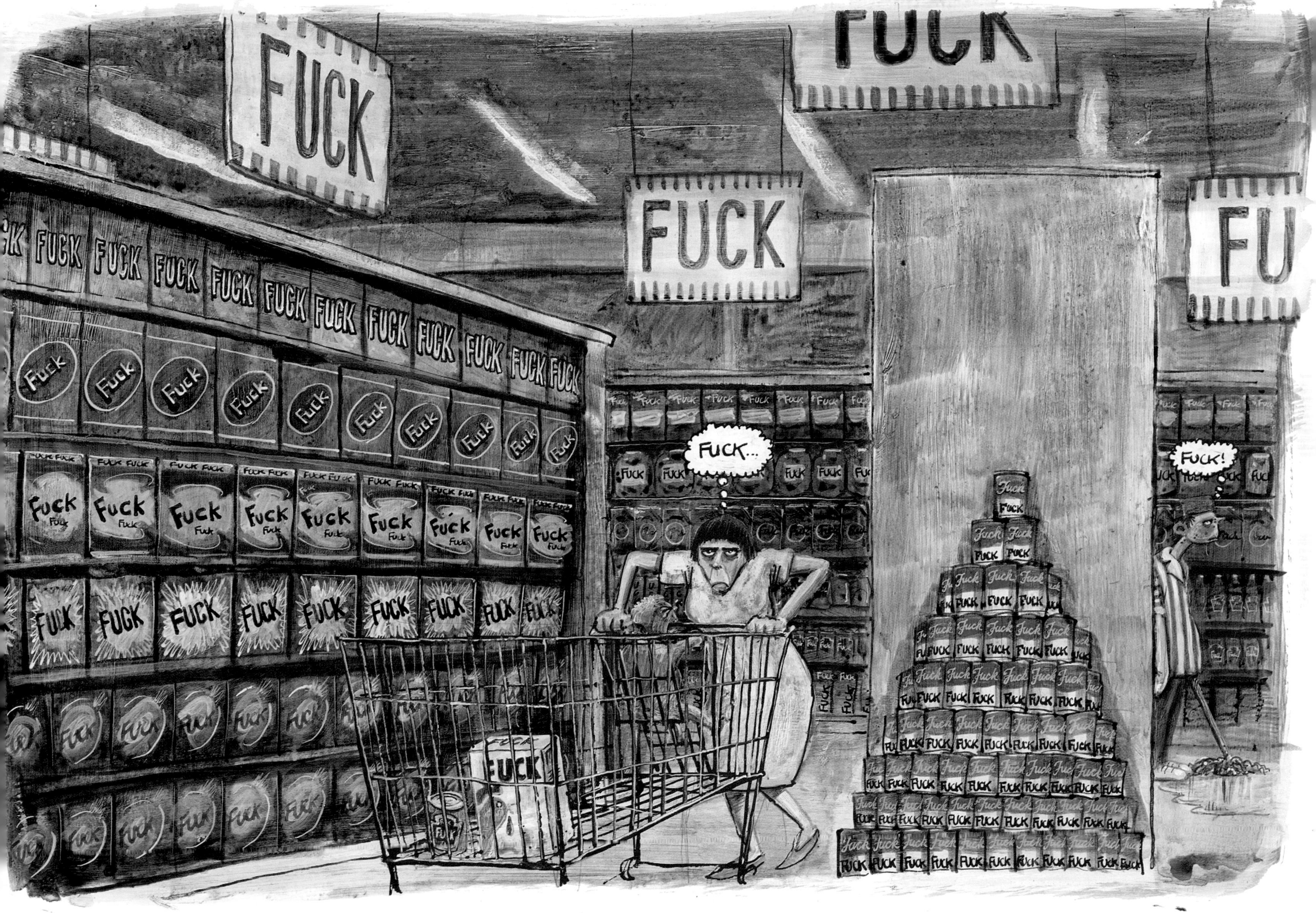
FUCK
FUCK
FUCK
FU
FUCK...
FUCK!

The Conquest of Space

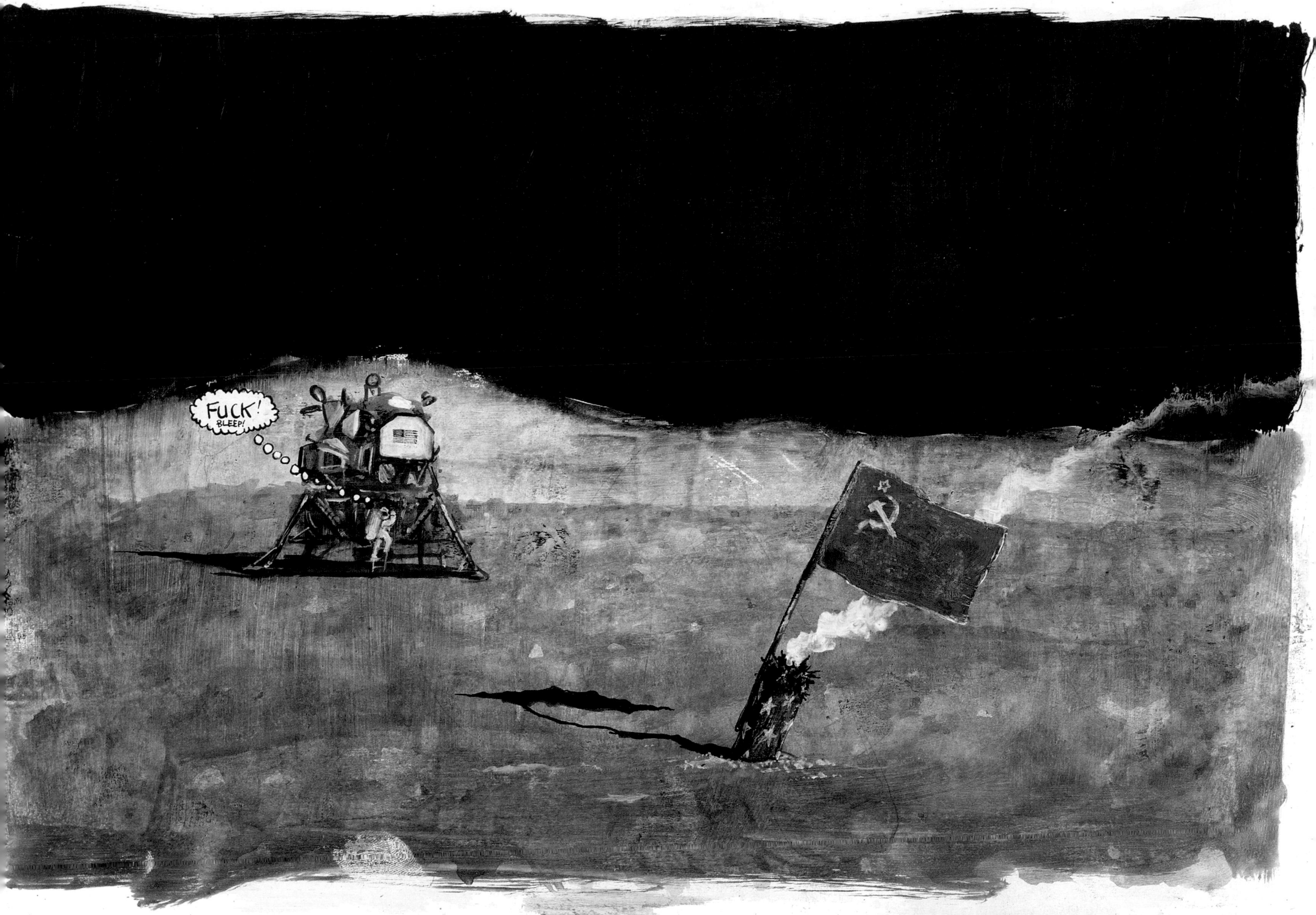
FUCK!
BLEEP!

Democracy in Action

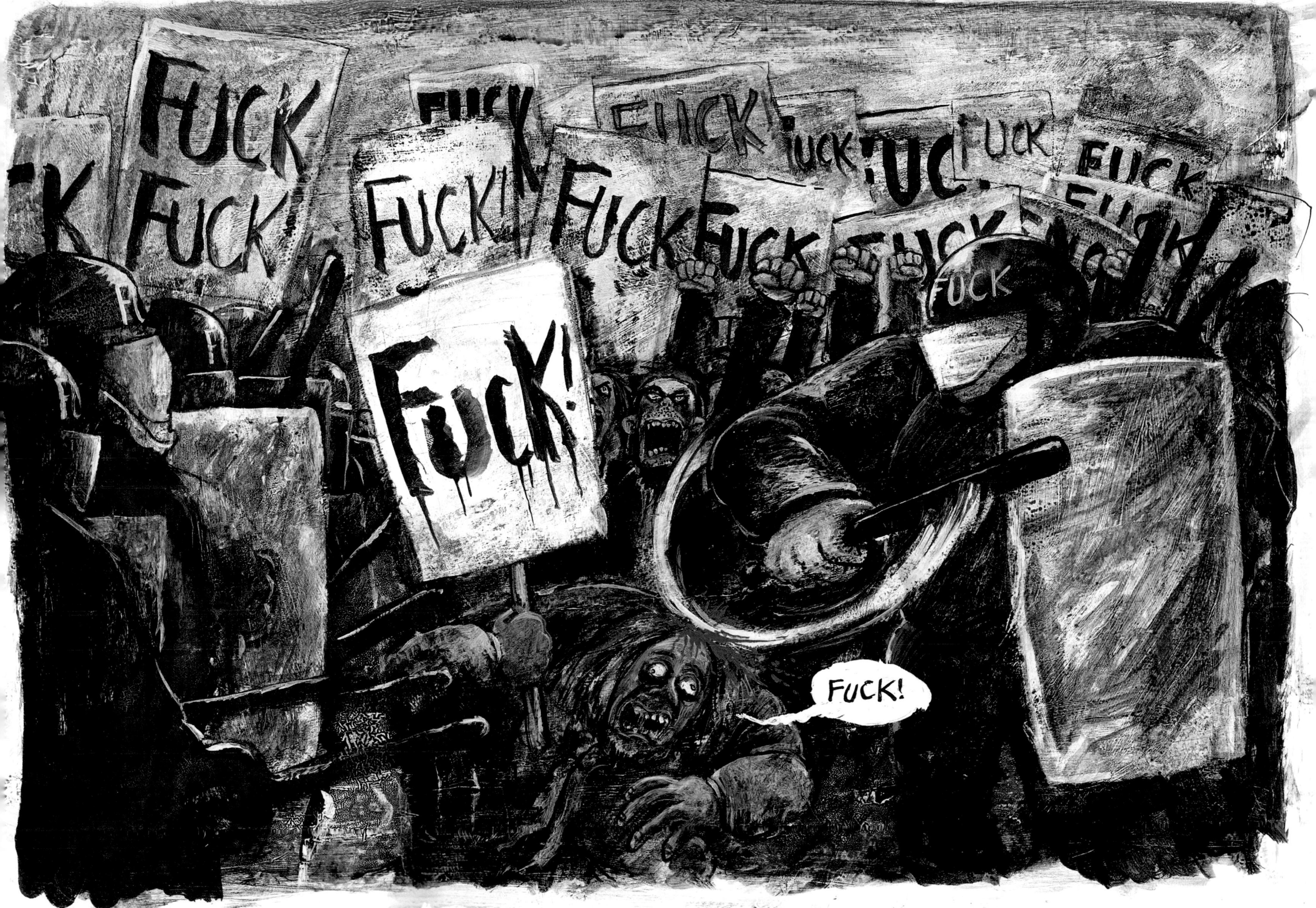
FUCK
FUCK
FUCK!
FUCK
FUCK
FUCK!
FUCK
FUCK!

Live Aid

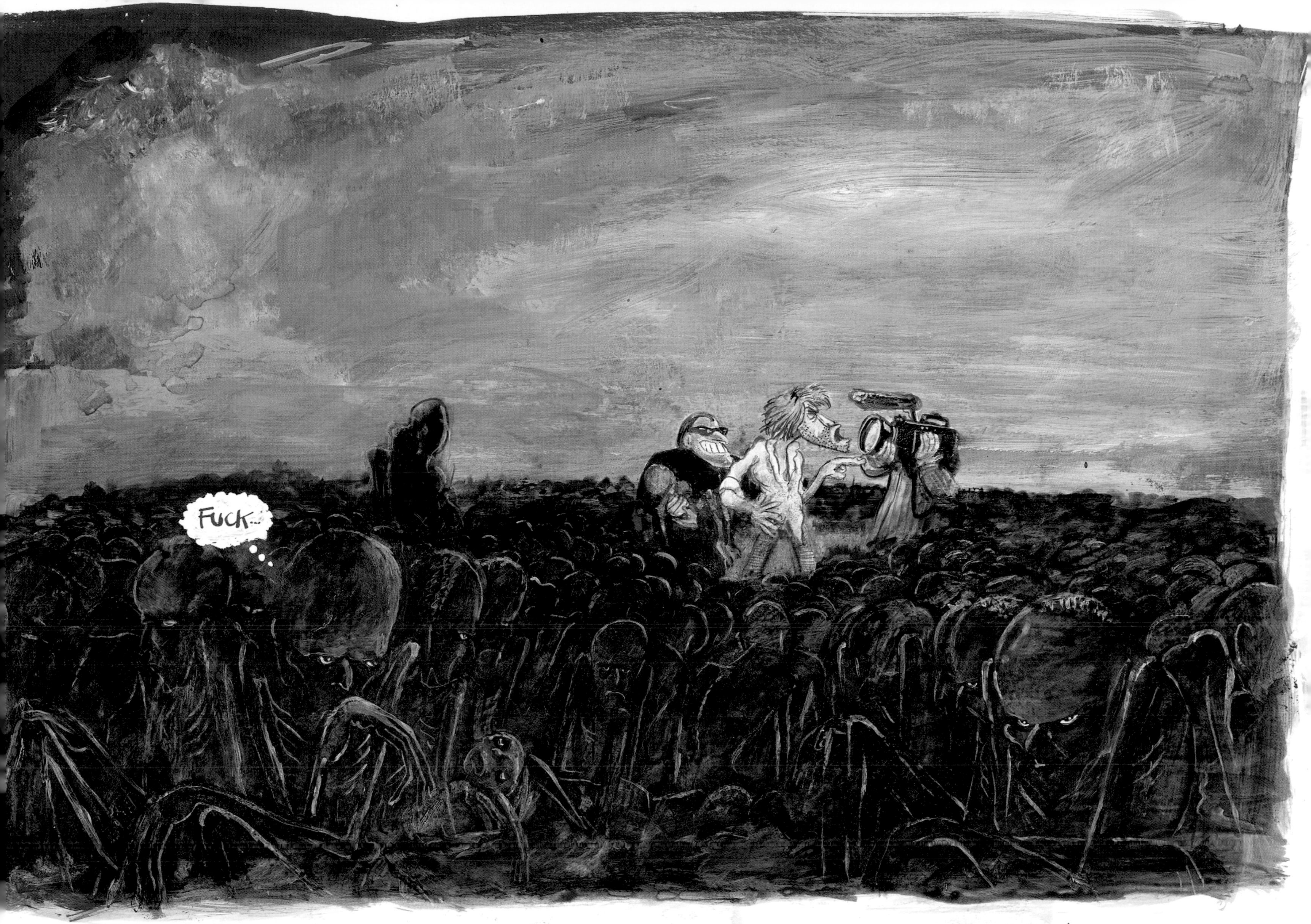
FUCK...

The Developing World

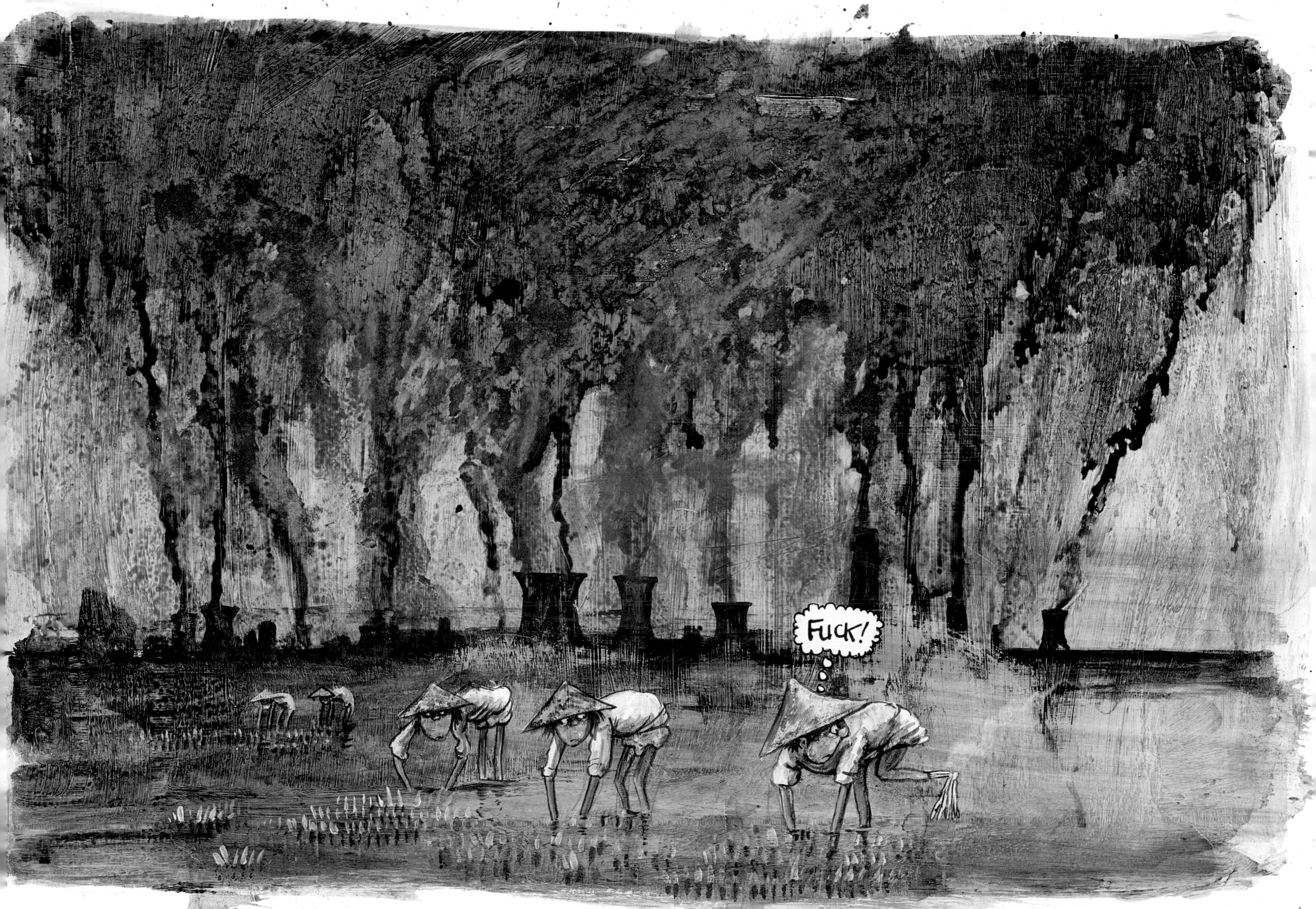
FUCK!

9/11

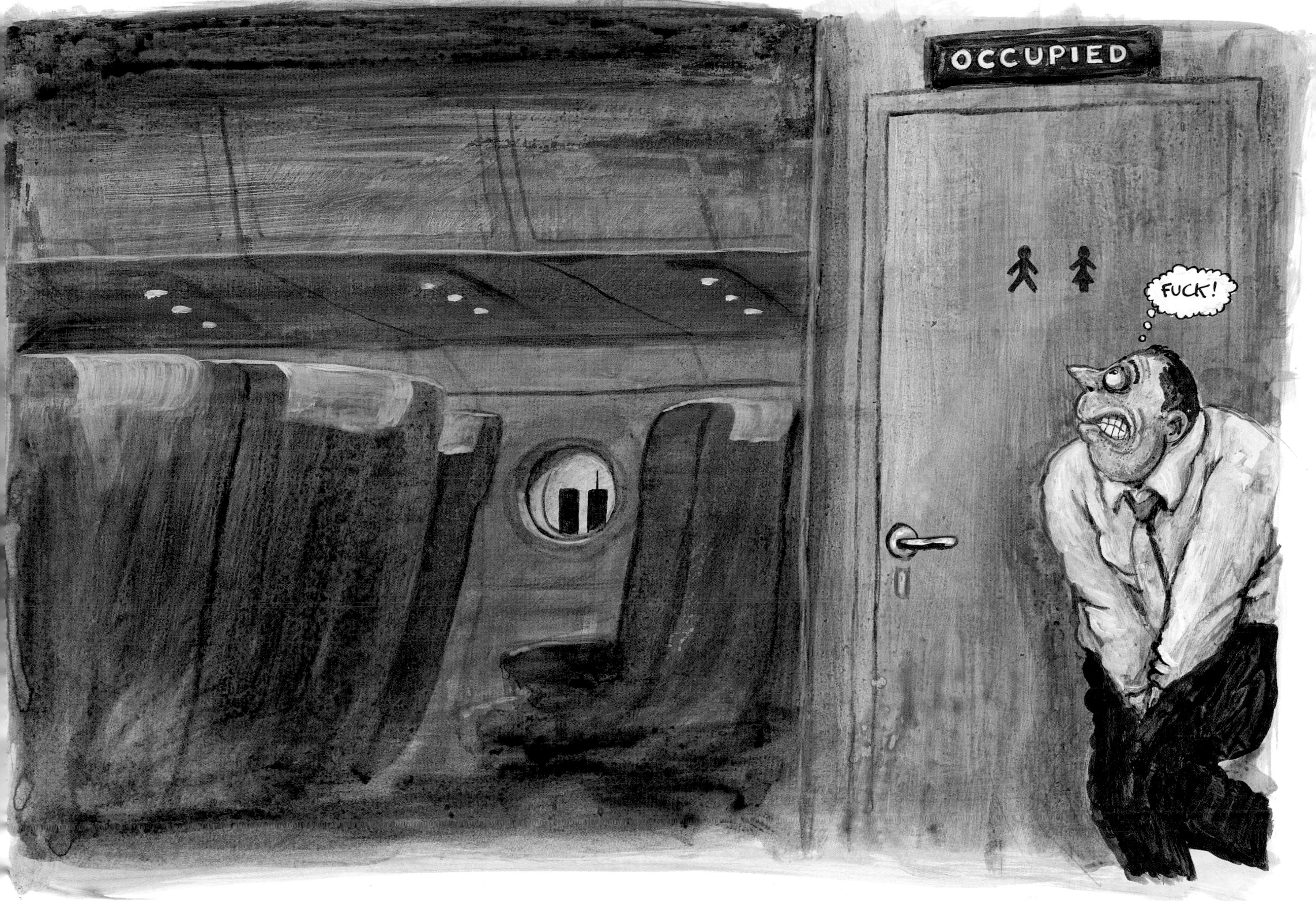
OCCUPIED
FUCK!

Humanitarian Interventionism

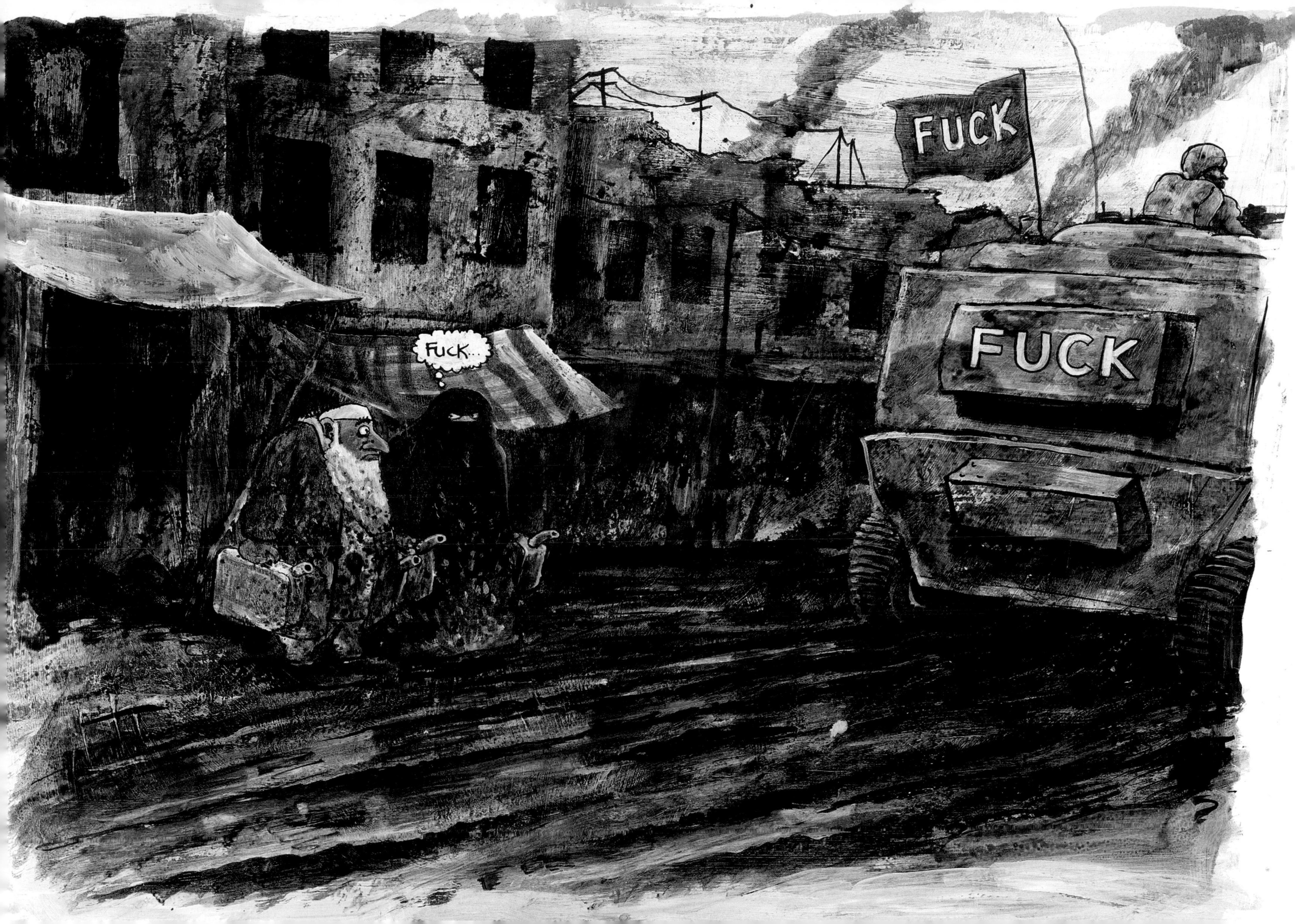
FUCK...
FUCK
FUCK

The War on Terror

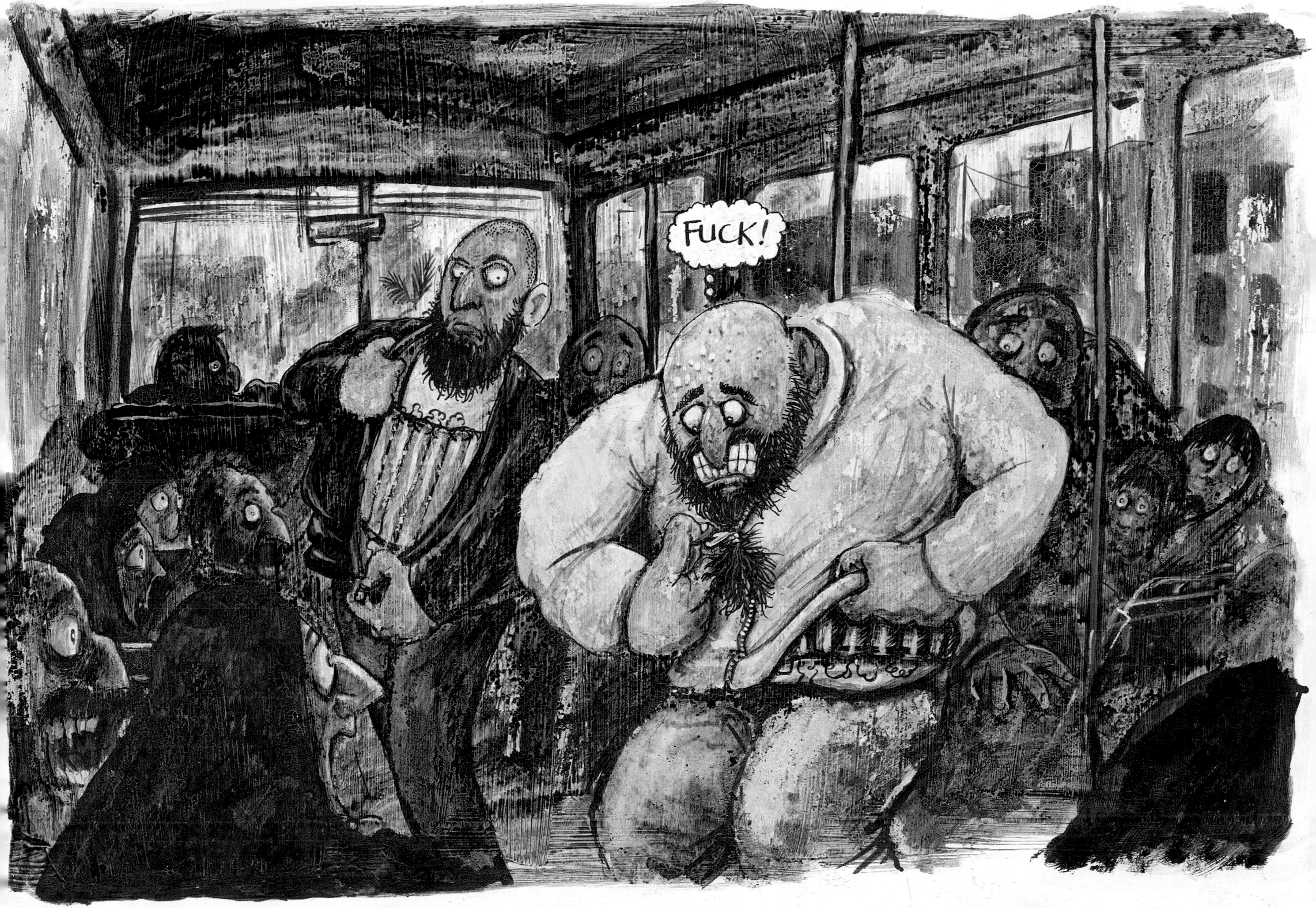
FUCK!

The Information Revolution

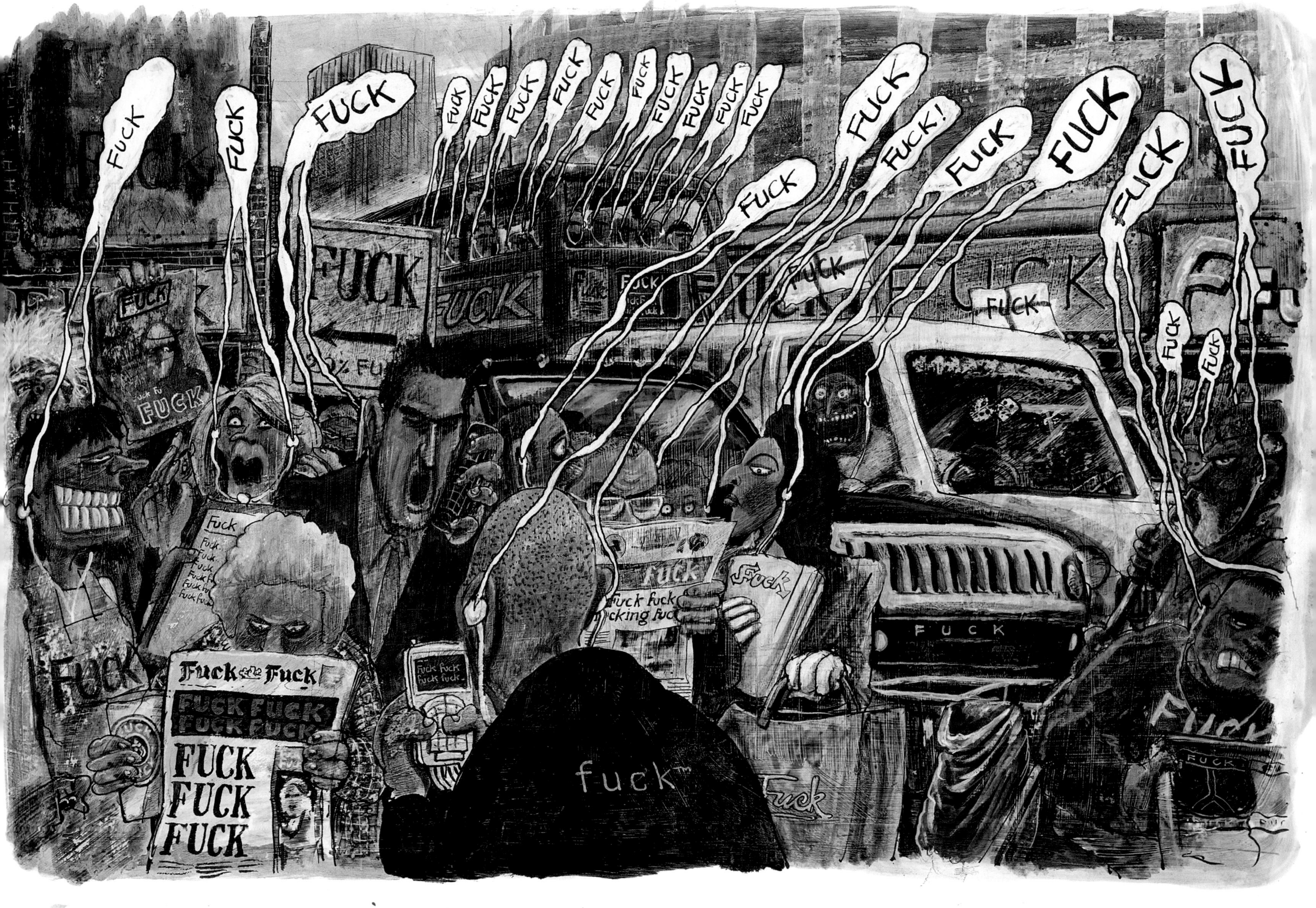

FUCK
FUCK
FUCK
FUCK
FUCK
FUCK
FUCK
FUCK
FUCK
FUCK
FUCK
FUCK
FUCK
FUCK
FUCK!
FUCK
FUCK
FUCK
FUCK
FUCK
FUCK
FUCK
FUCK
FUCK
FUCK
FUCK
FUCK
Fuck
FUCK
Fuck
FUCK
Fuck
Fuck fuck
fuck fuck
Fuck the Fuck
FUCK FUCK
FUCK FUCK
FUCK
FUCK
FUCK
fuck™
Fuck

Globalization

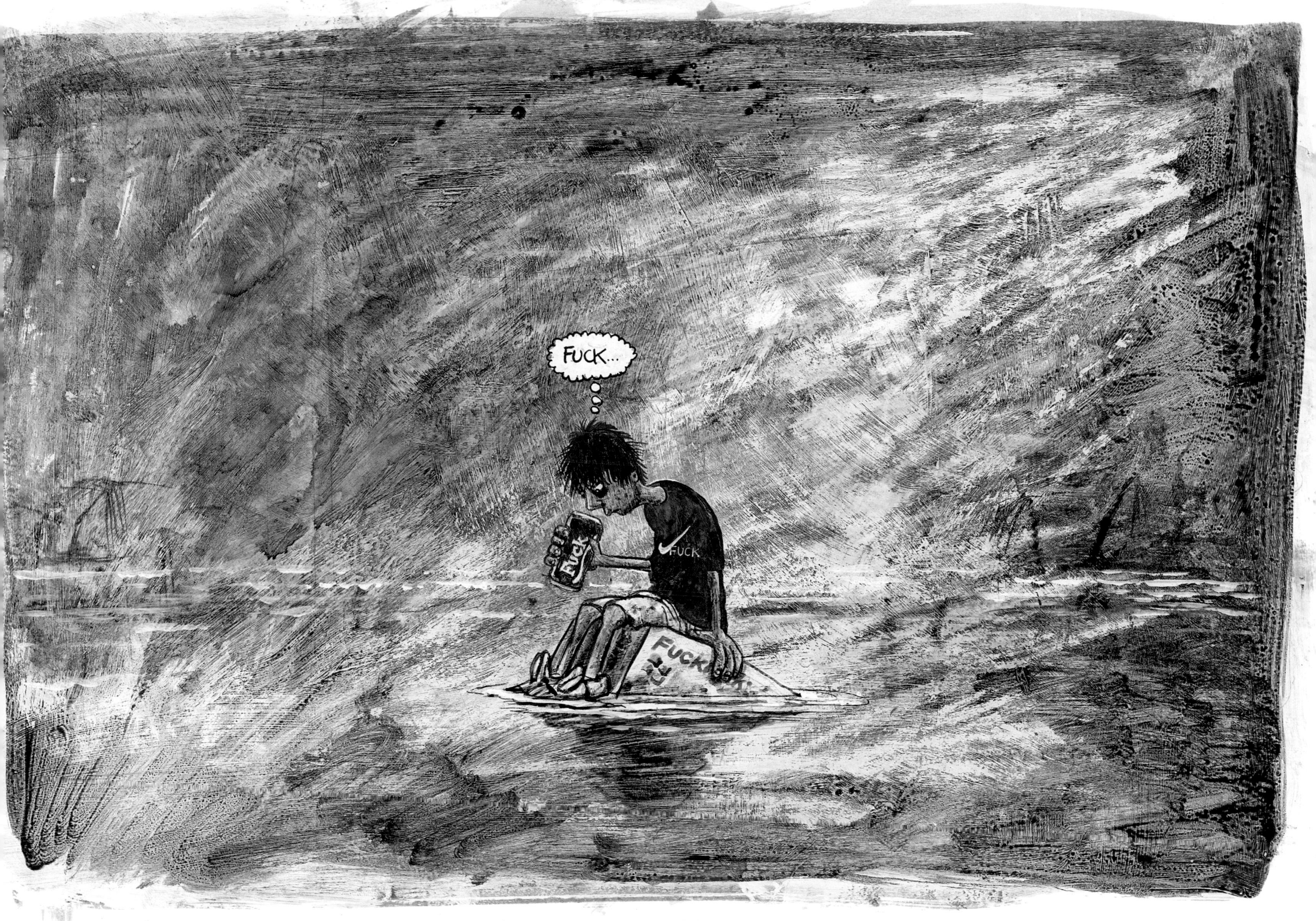
FUCK...
FUCK
FUCK
FUCK

Man Harnesses the Power of Genetics

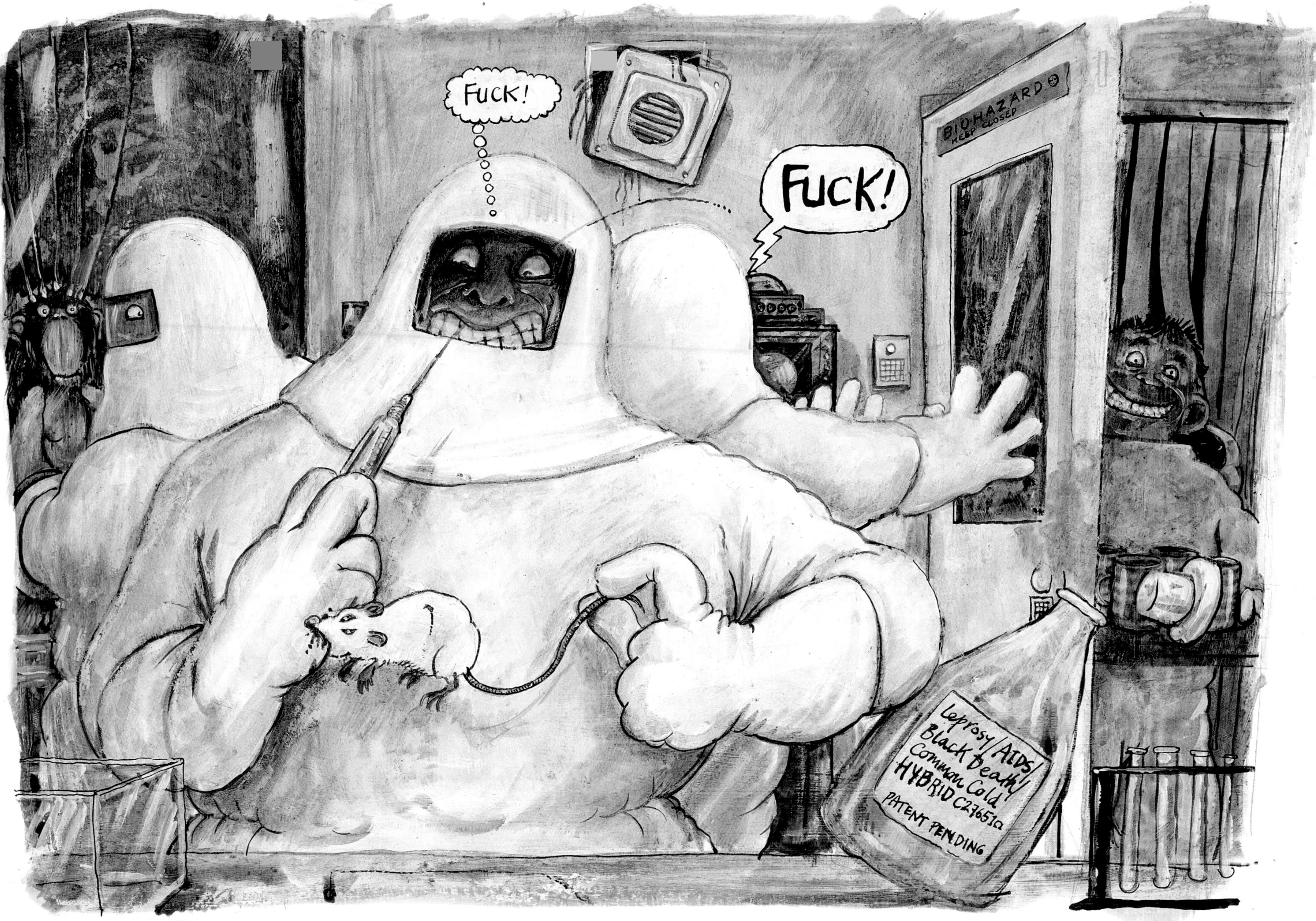
FUCK!
FUCK!
BIOHAZARD
KEEP CLOSED
Leprosy/AIDS/
Black Death/
Common Cold
HYBRID C27651a
PATENT PENDING

A New Ecology

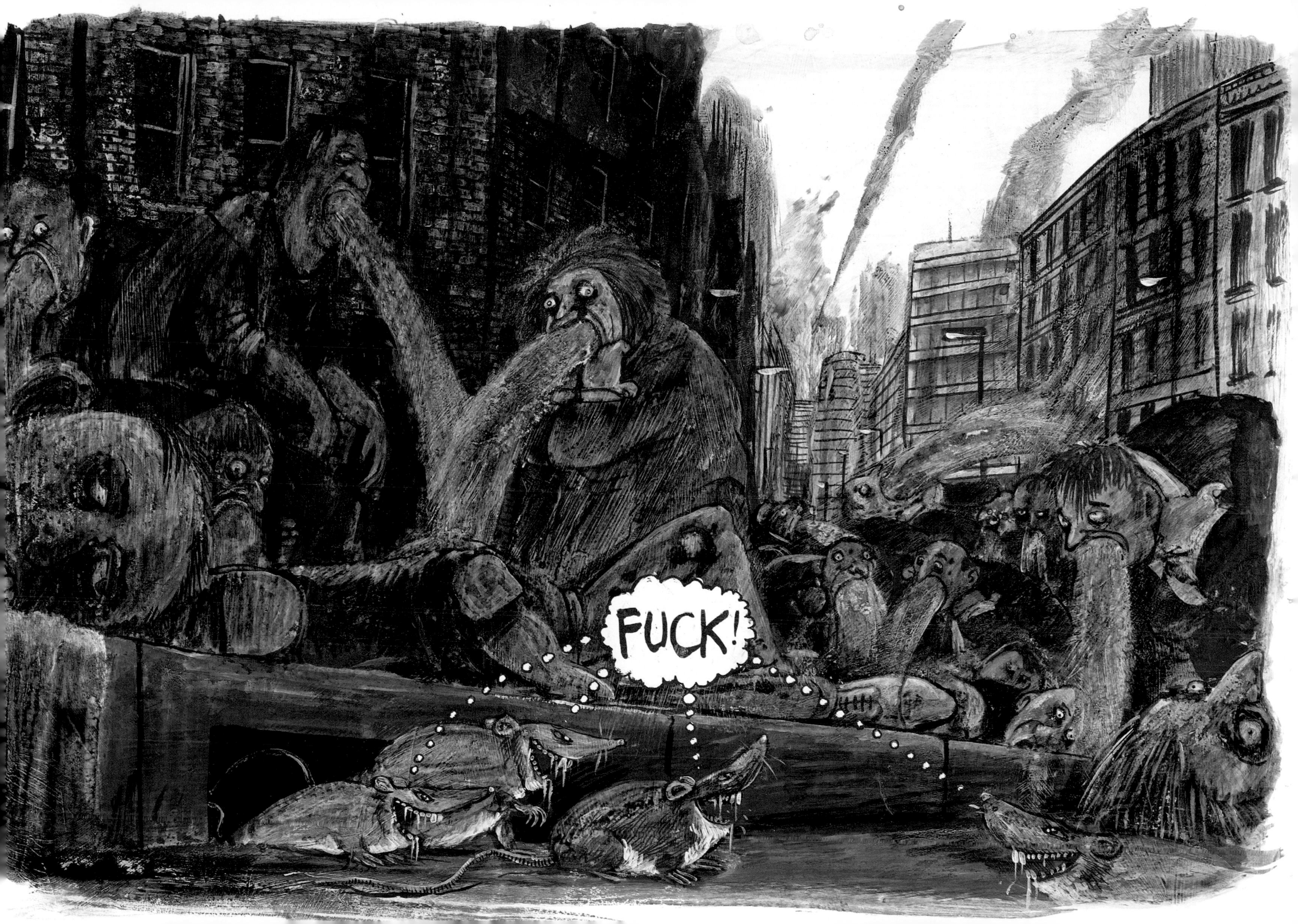
FUCK!

Human Evolution and the Long Awaited Second Coming of Christ

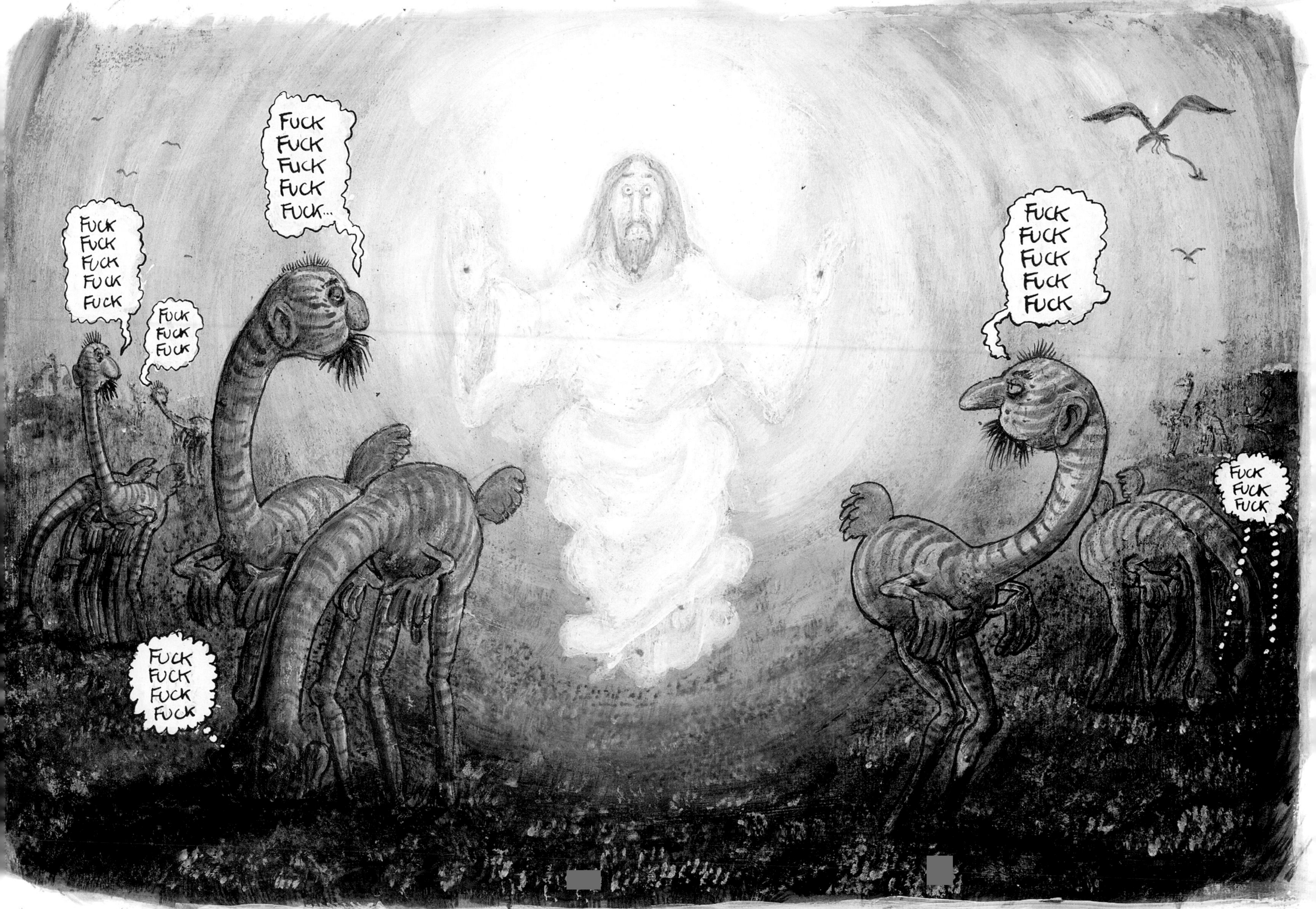
FUCK FUCK FUCK FUCK FUCK
FUCK FUCK FUCK
FUCK FUCK FUCK FUCK FUCK...
FUCK FUCK FUCK FUCK
FUCK FUCK FUCK FUCK FUCK
FUCK FUCK FUCK

The End

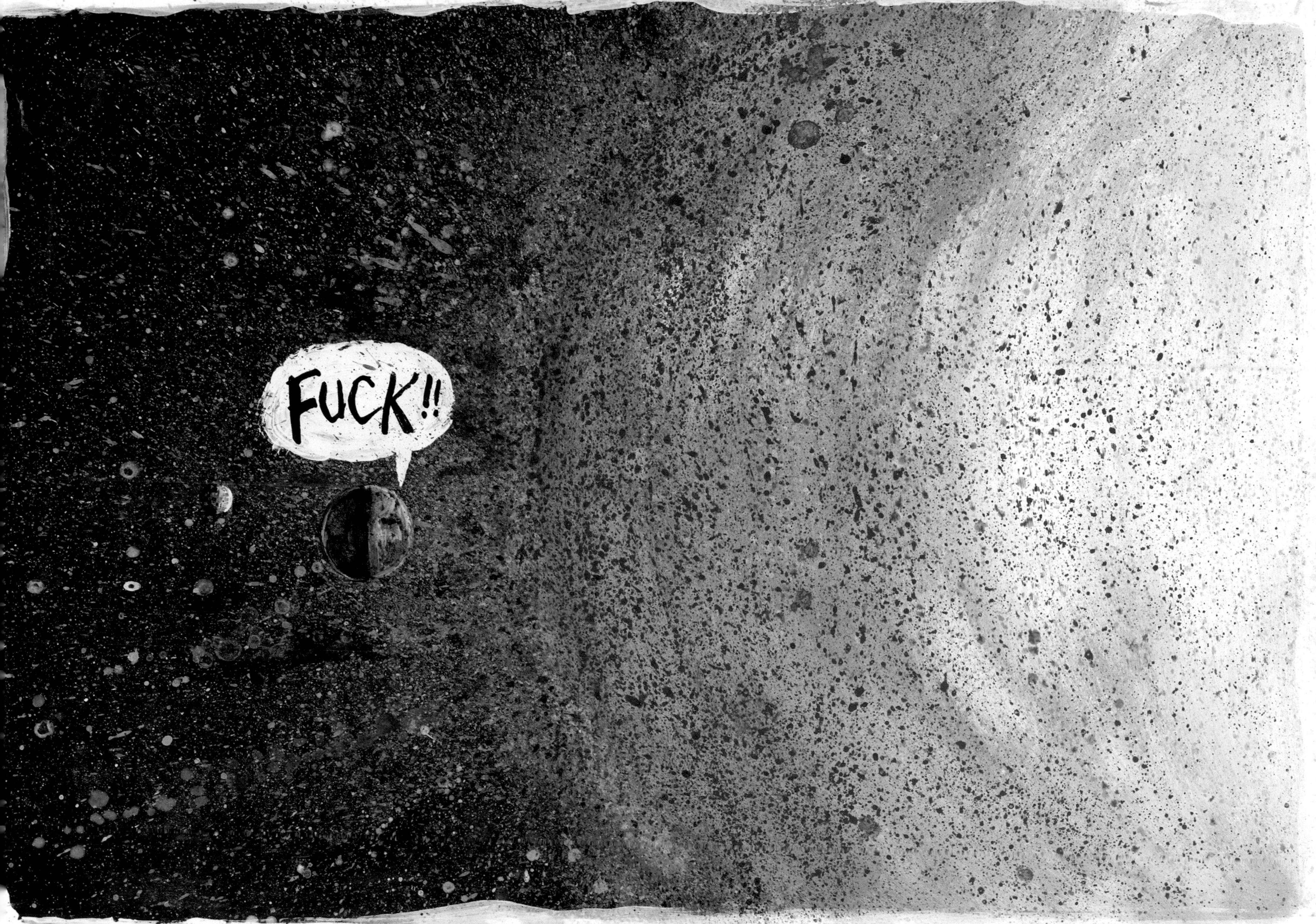
FUCK!!

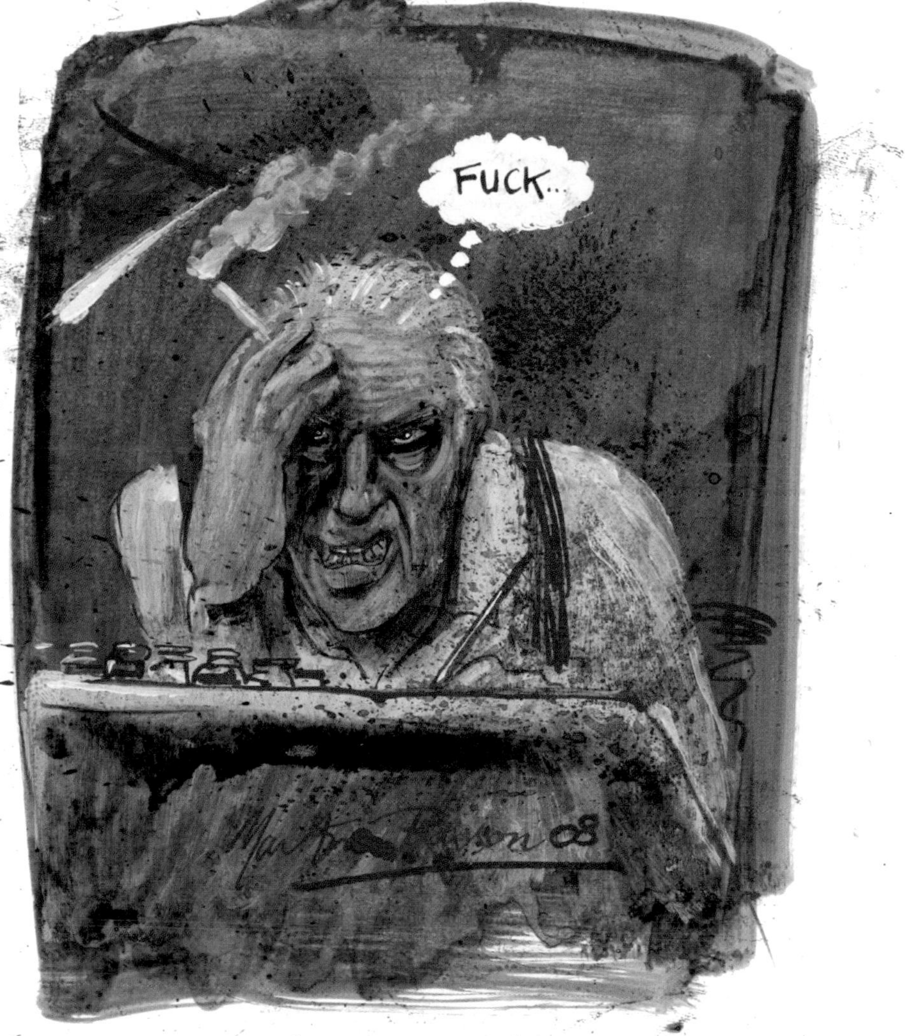
FUCK..

Martin Rowson is an award-winning political cartoonist whose work appears regularly in the *Guardian*, the *Independent on Sunday*, the *Daily Mirror*, the *Scotsman*, *Tribune*, *Index on Censorship*, thc *Morning Star* and *The Spectator*. His previous publications include comic-book adaptations of *The Waste Land* and *Tristram Shandy*, a novel, *Snatches* (2006), and a memoir, *Stuff* (2007). He lives with his wife and their two teenage children in south-east London.